KHUSHWANT SINGH
IN WISDOM & IN JEST

Vijay Narain Shankar
Onkar Singh

Vitasta

Published by
Renu Kaul Verma for
Vitasta Publishing Pvt Ltd
2/15, Ansari Road, Daryaganj
New Delhi - 110 002
info@vitastapublishing.com

ISBN 978-93-86473-10-3

Cover and layout by Vits Press
Printed by Vikas Computer and Printers, New Delhi

For my wife
Brinda
&
daughters
Tanya and Lara
—Vijay N. Shankar

For my wife
Vichitra,
daughter Nityashjit Kaur
and my *nati* Sonit Chaudhary
—Onkar Singh

Khushwant Singh wrote by hand, usually with an ink pen, as he sprawled on a sofa before the fireplace and put his legs up on a 'moorha' He wrote like this for most of the day

Contents

The Rainbow Man

Unquestionably the most popular ever writer in India, Khushwant Singh was an enigma. To everyone who knew him or read him. And to himself too. An enigma of contradictions, a mixture of everything that makes life enthralling and sad and joyful and without boundaries.

He was the Rainbow Man who had in him all the colours of existence, the dark, the bright, the deep and the light. Here, in this book, we have endeavoured to bring the rainbow into our pages. I met him for an interview when he was in his mid seventies. "what is it about ?" Khushwant asked.

"About you," I said. "For the 'personality' page in the magazine."

"Don't make a fuss about me," he said. "No fuss," I said. "People like to get stuff on you. Can't get enough of you." He shrugged it off. But I think he loved what I said. It was true enough. People loved what he did, what he said and what he wrote. They still do and that's what this book is all about.

Vijay Narain Shankar

Acknowledgements

Writing a book is always hard work but it became a pleasure writing about Khushwant because of the readiness with which people came forward to talk about him.

There was something they all had in common. A great and lasting love for Khushwant. He was not just a famous writer, prominent editor, prolific columnist, and a stormy petrel of the literary scene; he was unforgettable.

Our heartfelt thanks to editors Kuldip Nayyar and H K Dua; authors and journalists Sir Mark Tully, Kumkum Chadha, Chandni Luthra, Suneet Veer Singh; Khushwant's friends Soli Sorabjee and F S Aijazuddin; film-maker Bobby Bedi who filmed Khushwant's novel, *Train To Pakistan*; artist Arpana Caur and writer Ajeet Caur; hotelier and close Khushwant family friend, Mrs Charanji Singh, scholar Amarpreet Singh Gill and the late Supercop K P S Gill

This book would not have been possible without the

assistance we received from Khushwant's daughter, Mala Singh Dayal, and son, Rahul Singh, both authors and media personalities.

A word of thanks to my (Vijay Narain Shankar) old friend Montek Singh Ahluwalia who introduced the book pre-publication, at the Khushwant Singh Litfest at Kasauli in August, 2016.

We thank the dynamic Renu Kaul Verma, Managing Director of Vitasta Publishing, for working with us from the inception of this book and bringing it to readers.

Thanks are also due to Tanya Berry for having undertaken the daunting job of doing the second proof reading of the book apart from the professional proofing. A fine job of editing was done by Bill Koul for which, many thanks.

Foreword

'No point in writing if you're not honest,' my father always said.

–Rahul Singh

Just when my father had turned 99, the Department of English and Cultural Studies of Punjab University devoted a whole day to discuss him and his writings. In his typical self-deprecatory style, he wrote to them that there were many more eminent writers than him who deserved the honour more. 'I am a mere scribbler whose scribbles some people like and enjoy', he said. 'However, I have just entered my 100th year and I believe that I have managed to write over 50 books.'

He also probably had the longest continuously running weekly column of any writer. He began it when he took over the editorship of *The Illustrated Weekly of India* in 1969. After he left the weekly, or rather was fired from the weekly, he continued it in other publications, mainly the *Hindustan Times*, of which he was also the editor. That makes over half a century of the column, which he titled, *'With Malice towards One and All'*. It had a cartoon by Mario Miranda, the late cartoonist who used to work with him in the weekly, with him sitting in a light bulb, pen in one hand and glass of Scotch whiskey in the other. When he first became the editor of *The Illustrated Weekly*, its circulation was around 65,000. When he left ten years later, it had crossed 450,000, making it by far the most read news weekly in the country. Some of the young journalists, who worked under him, like MJ Akbar and Bachi Karkaria, later became big names in the journalistic profession. Part of the success of the weekly was due to the cover stories that he often carried on various Indian communities, copies of which were lapped by members of that community.

'We are such a wonderfully varied, vibrant and colourful nation that we should all feel privileged to be Indians', he once said. *'I certainly do, despite the many frustrations and shortcomings that we face,'* he had continued. *'But we are still largely ignorant about each other. Look at the disgraceful way those from the north-east, our fellow Indians, are treated in some parts of the country, even today, made fun of and discriminated against.'*

My father's main aim in his writings has been to inform,

provoke and occasionally raise a laugh. He believed that we took ourselves much too seriously and there is also a great deal of humbug and hypocrisy around; so-called godmen, astrologers, faith healers and the like were constantly making fools of us; and we spent too much time in worthless rituals and were prey to superstition. He always believed that worship was not work; but it was work that was worship.

'Love the Lord...of all religions'

Though he was an agnostic, he was also proud to be a Sikh. He admitted it was something of a contradiction–he believed strongly in the sense of Sikh identity, of Sikhs retaining their symbols of the turban, long hair and the beard. Without that, he was convinced that the Sikh religion would eventually die out and perhaps merge with Hinduism. He knew that many Sikhs, perhaps even a majority of them, had discarded these symbols of the Sikh identity. That was something the Sikh leadership should discuss and ponder over. Nevertheless, he was appalled over *'Operation Bluestar'* and opposed Jarnail Singh Bhindranwale, though he wished more Sikhs had also done so.

'I rarely go to a gurdwara, yet I study all religions', he liked to say. *'There is a poem called Abou Ben Adhem, which represents much of how I felt towards religion. I will summarise it. Abou Ben Adhem awakes one evening and finds an angel in his room, writing in a book of gold. "What are you writing?" he asks the angel.*

The angel replies, "The names of all those who love the Lord." "Is mine there?" asks Abou Ben Adhem. "No", replies the angel." "Then", says Abou Ben Adhem, "put me down as one who loves his fellow men". The angel returns the next evening and tells Abou Ben Adhem that he is on the very top of the list.'

So, my father would say, *"Be like Abou Ben Adhem. Love your fellow human beings. Loving your Lord, no matter of which religion, is less important."'*

What disturbed him most in his last days was the growth of intolerance and of fundamentalism in all religions, including his own—Sikhism, Islam and Hinduism. He felt we must combat this menace if we were to develop and grow as a progressive, peaceful and secular society. He had hopes in our new and young generation, who were better educated and more aware of what was going on in the world. Mobile phones, Twitter, Facebook, of which he knew nothing and which come under the umbrella of social media, were, he believed, helping in this process.

He had several concerns. The two most important concerns being: (a) the education and welfare of the girl child, which we had neglected; and (b) the ecology and the environment, which we had degraded and abused. He often said he had been fortunate enough to have spent a lot of time in Kasauli in a house that his late wife (my mother) had inherited from her parents. It is part of a cantonment and the military has kept it in a pristine condition. He wished more parts of India had been kept like that.

When he turned 99, he used to tell people that he was at the sunset of his life, which he had lived to the full, with few regrets. He repeatedly said that he was a proud Sikh and, above all, a proud Indian of a great, though often bewildering, nation.

As for my father's frankness and also boldness, the best I can do is to quote the following, in his own words, from some of his writings that I have rummaged through.

'My mother tongue is English, though my mother can't speak a word of it.'

'When anyone asks me, *"what is your mother tongue?"*, I reply without hesitation, *"English"*. They regard my swarthy complexion, the turban on my head and my greying beard. The contemptuous look in their eyes leaves me in no doubt that they see me as the leftover of the breed of toadying spittle lickers of the British. When I add, *"My mother tongue is English, though my mother cannot speak one word of it,"* they roar with laughter. They think it is a big joke. How can a black man born in India, deriving the sustenance from the dung heap of a Punjabi village, describe English as his mother tongue except in jest?

'I do not jest. I call English my mother tongue because I am more familiar with it than with any other language. Since most people I mix with are also more at ease with English than with what they call their mother tongues, I hear more

English spoken than any other language. All my work is done in English. I write it better than my three Indian languages, Punjabi, Hindi and Urdu. I know that in writing English, I make errors in grammar and my vocabulary is limited. I try to better my diction, improve my syntax and endeavour to turn out a polished sentence, which is at once pregnant with meaning and pleasing to the ear. With me English is a passion. No other language gives me quite the same pleasure. I find it more musical and much richer in its literature than any other language of the world.

When I make these assertions, my friends shake their heads, cluck their tongues and remark, *'Even if all you say about English is true, it still does not make it your mother tongue.'*

I bark back, *'So much the worse for definitions! If a person cannot speak the language spoken by his mother (not an inconceivable situation, for example, children of Indian parents in England or even children in westernised Bombay and Delhi) it is a travesty of fact to describe that language as a mother tongue. Let us redefine it as the language one is most at home with and which one loves. So defined, Jawaharlal Nehru's mother tongue was English. His daughter, Indira Gandhi's mother tongue is also English. And it is also mine.'*

'India is where I will live and die.'

'Why am I an Indian?' I did not have any choice–I was born one. If the good Lord had consulted me on the subject,

I might have chosen a country more affluent, less crowded, less censorious in matters of food and drink, unconcerned with personal equations and free of religious bigotry.

'Am I proud of being an Indian?' I can't really answer this one. I can scarcely take credit for the achievements of my forefathers. And I have little to be proud of what we are doing today. On balance, I would say, *'No, I am not proud of being an Indian.'*

'Why don't you get out and settle in some other country?' Once again, I have very little choice. All the countries I might like to live in have restricted quotas for emigrants. Most of them are white and have a prejudice against coloured people. In any case, I feel more relaxed and at home in India.

I dislike many things in my country, mostly the government. I know the government is not the same thing as the country, but it never stops trying to appear in that garb. This is where I belong and this is where I intend to live and die. Of course, I like going abroad. Living is easier, the wine and food are better, the women more forthcoming – it's more fun. However, I soon get tired of all those things and want to get back to my dung-heap and be among my loud-mouthed, sweaty, smelly countrymen. I am like my kinsmen in Africa, England and elsewhere. My head tells me it is better to live abroad, my belly tells me it is more fulfilling to be in 'phoren', but my heart tells me 'get back to India'. Each time I return home, and drive through the stench of bare-bottomed defecators that line the road from Santa Cruz airport to the city, I ask myself:

Breathes there the man with soul so dead;
Who never to himself hath said;
This is my own, my native land!

I can scarcely breathe, but I yell, *'Yeah, this is my native land. I don't like it but I love it.'*

'Are you an Indian first and a Punjabi or Sikh second? Or, is it the other way round?' I don't like the way these questions are framed and if I am denied my Punjabiness or my community tradition, I would refuse to call myself Indian. I am Indian, Punjabi and Sikh. And even so, I have a patriotic kinship with one who says, *'I am Indian, Hindu and Haryanvi'* or one who says, *'I am Indian, Moplah Muslim and Malayli'*. I want to retain my religious and linguistic identity, without making them exclusive in any way.

'Our diversity is our strength'

I am convinced that our guaranteed diversity is our strength. As soon as you try to obliterate regional language in favour of one national language or religion, in the name of one Indian credo, you will destroy the unity of the country. Twice was our Indianness challenged–in 1962 by the Chinese and in 1965 by the Pakistanis. Then, despite our many differences of language, religion and faith, we rose as one to defend our country. In the ultimate analysis, it is the consciousness of frontiers that makes a nation. We have proved that we are one nation. What then is this talk of Indianising people who are already Indian? And has anyone any right to arrogate to himself the right to decide who is and who is not a good Indian?

'If you write fearlessly and candidly, you have to be prepared to pay the price. And there's no point in writing if you're not honest. I've always written what I felt and believed to be true. There's no secret I kept to myself. At times this has upset people but I've never been bothered.'

Boldness

My father was a great defender of secularism and human rights till the end. He waged a war against religious fundamentalism. In his own words:

'One of the regrets in my life is that I could have played a bigger role in my battle against the fundoos. I should have written more against fundamentalists. My battle is against fundoos from all communities. I have spoken out against Muslim religious fundamentalists, against Hindu fundamentalists. Today, fundamentalists burn books they do not like, they beat up journalists who write against them, they attack cinema houses showing films they do not approve of, they pervert texts from history books, they foul mouth everyone who disagrees with them. If we love our country we have to save it from communal forces.'

For these beliefs, especially those he held against the brand of Sikh extremism promoted by Jarnail Singh Bhindranwale, he received death threats and assassins were despatched to eliminate him. But he refused to be cowed down.

Though he was an agnostic, he was proud to be a Sikh and took a deep interest in all the religions and could quote from the *Koran*, the *Gita*, the *Bible* and the *Granth Sahib*. And curiously enough, the two persons he most admired were both people of faith, Mahatma Gandhi and Mother Teresa. After he had written a piece on Mother Teresa for the *New York Times*, she wrote him a short note of thanks, which became one of his most prized possessions: *'I am told you do not believe in God,'* she wrote. *'I send you God's blessings.'*

Rahul Singh
June 2017

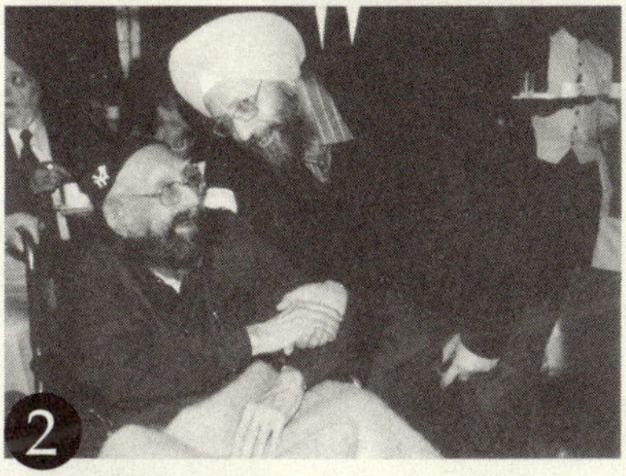

1 Khushwant Singh with then President Abdul Kalam who visited the writer at his house

2 With veteran journalist, Onkar Sing, co-author of this book

3 With Meridian chairperson Charanjit Kaur standing next to cake that former President Abdul Kalam sent for his birthday

4 With old friend, Punjabi author Ajeet Kaur

5 Though he stubbornly justified the Emergency, Khushwant joined editors in a protest at gagging of the Press.

6 He kept up with his swimming and tennis as long as he could. Seen here during a match with none other than Leander Paes.

7 Editor at work. He became an editor who was known to every reader and few editors have had the kind of success that Khushwant had

8 Those were the days....Khushwant with wife Kawal

Stories all his life

And life was a story of wonder and challenges

Every day of his life, Khushwant Singh spun stories from the things he saw and felt around him and had readers waiting for more. He was the witness and also the prosecution for everything that he thought, using his favourite words—'a humbug.' Everything was judged in a clear prism of his common sense, for common sense, at its best, is true wisdom. Nothing that was awry was accepted and it was strange that people enjoyed getting ticked off by the indomitable Sardar. They did not challenge him but they agreed with him. That is the dilemma of traditional India. The reason he was so widely read was because he told good stories, in his fiction as well as in his columns, and held the reader's interest. The storyteller reveals the extreme possibilities of peoples' lives and connects the reader to strange realities, so that they can make sense of their own lives. In his stories, of real and imaginary people, he had always something to give by way of the romance of unusual.

The profound and the profane

Khushwant was a man who lived and wrote amidst the spaces of the sublime and the ridiculous. Working in complete and fearless acceptance of his own nature, without pretence or hypocrisy, he wrote as he thought and always maintained, 'I did not care a damn for what people thought or said.' There is a unique and surprising diversity in the range of his writing. From a seminal work on the Sikh history, translations on the Sikh scriptures and the Hindu Upanishads, short stories, novels, presentations of Urdu poetry which he loved, to essays and inspirational books and finally to his much loved and also much criticised joke books, Khushwant had done it all. 'I do not stick to any one style or genre,' he once said to me in one of the many interviews we had over the course of many decades. 'I do not like to be trapped in anything. Look around you at nature. Nature has no style and no genre. Nature makes mountains and trees and rivers, snakes and insects and elephants and giraffes. Creativity should be free and must not be limited except by one's own mind and thinking.'

Khushwant wrote in the realms of the profound as well as the profane. One was derived from his tremendous humour and carefree nature. 'I am an incorrigible jester,' he used to say. More than other men, Khushwant had a secret life that was lived away from the media blast and the applause. Certainly, he loved and revelled in the applause and made no bones about it. He was a latecomer to success and was hungry for it. For the first 40 years of his life, he had wandered the labyrinths of an unsettled, often despairing life. He took up jobs and dropped them, he tried his hand at various things, he took up briefless barrister, but his real calling eluded him for the most part of his youth.

The last time we met Khushwant was after the release of his book, *The Khushwant Nama*, a bit grandly titled in the style of the life histories of the Mogul emperors. It was strange that, in spite of his phenomenal success in being India's most popular and most discussed writer, someone who had written over 90 books and ran columns in nearly 50 newspapers, he still was unhappy about the fact that his last and most ambitious novel, *Delhi*, had been indifferently received. It was a historical novel, set on a magnificent scale, and written with some beautiful passages based on the poetry and the cultural heritage of the city that he loved but, as a novel, it did not hold attention.

'The greater the artist,' wrote Nobel prize winning author, Ben Okri, '...the greater the imagination, the greater the will, and the greater the sense of secret failure.'

He was 98 years old at the time, and the success and the applause were all behind him. It was important for him to know that the writing had been good, for he was the quintessential writer, and at the end of the day what mattered were the wisdom and the truth that had come from his pen. He spoke about the new writers, such as Jhumpa Lahiri, Amitav Ghosh, Arundhati Roy and others, praising their turn of phrase and thought content, and then said, 'but I belong to the old school. Mulk Raj Anand, RK Narayan etc and I think I write as well as them.'

The media was quick to brand him with controversy and shock, for it is the loud and clamourous voice that sells. People who never read him, or ever would, knew him only as a jester and a columnist. He was called 'the Indian gad fly' as an intended compliment; and also a 'dirty old man', perhaps also as a compliment. In his own carefree way, Khushwant enjoyed that, because he took neither himself nor other people too seriously. Yet, as writer Shoba De has said, he was none of those things.

A palette of everything

Khushwant was a gifted and sensitive writer who depicted the irony and the passions of life with his unbridled realism. Like Hemingway, Khushwant was Spartan with his words. He wrote but with the essence of what he saw. There was a restraint born of wisdom and understanding that life is as it is. The joy and the tragedy happen in a world of imperfect men, condemned to live unsteady passions. Indeed, if there were no imperfections in men and the lives they were given, there would be no stories. One could feel some of this on reading his book, *The Train to Pakistan*. The years before he wrote that first novel, of a struggle and a self-discovery, that a writer faces alone, are reflected in that book. He had done many things, given them up and yet almost inexorably, life had taken him somewhere.

In his late 30s, there was a time of doubt, a low point in his life. He was a rich man's son and had lived well, travelled abroad and been to the best colleges in India and England. He was married and had mostly been living off his father, Sir Sobha Singh. His wife was from a prominent family, a feeling that rankled him. Also, by then, he had done only those works and jobs that he had hated. As a lawyer, he had seen the futility and dishonesty that he felt prevailed in the profession. Instead of burying himself in law books and briefs, he was more interested in the stories of criminals. So he socialised and took up literary pursuits, started reading whatever he could find. Since he was in Lahore and friendly with people of literary tastes, he could satisfy his lifelong love for Urdu poetry. These were the things that interested him and not the legal profession. He was quick to see through things, impatient with pomposity and outspoken by nature.

Then came a time, when the depressed and feckless

middle aged Khushwant just did not know where he was going. In that state of angst and emptiness, Khushwant went to the Bangla Sahib gurdwara in Delhi one evening. He curled up against a wall, as the Gurbani was chanted at sunset and, as the story is told, he did not move from there the whole night. The man, who did not believe in God, just sat there in the silence of a sleeping temple to find some kind of awakening. And, perhaps in the first light of dawn, there was a direction, the magic of a new beginning. For soon after that, he began to do something that was alien to his education and professional training. He began to find his freedom and himself, as he laboured on his first novel. He was once asked about the gurudwara incident. 'It was one of those things...a contradiction,' he said, as a matter of fact. It was more than that, as we shall see later. He had worked out his own personal religion after thinking about these things all his life. And yet sometimes, all one's thinking becomes powerless in the face of circumstances.

A latecomer to writing

There was not much that Khushwant did in the first 40 years of his life but his writing career was definitely on the horizon, although slow in coming. Though he did stints as a lawyer and a bureaucrat, he was a man trying to find his way all the time. It is strange that he did things that he did not like for many years and was, in a sense, fighting other people's expectations as well as his own choices. At some point, in his mid-life, of experimenting with what his future life would be, he got drawn to books and the literature. The lawyer, who hated the court, started reading poetry and great contemporary writers, such as Somerset Maugham and Aldous Huxley, and the classics from Shakespeare and Walter Scott. During his years in London, at the Indian High Commission, he was drawn to the writers and poets that he met. The freedom and openness of his creative mind attracted the ingénue Khushwant, for it had a resonance in his own. Even though he was still a decade away from his own serious writing, he did write articles from time to time. He also went to social parties where he met the great contemporary poets of the time, such as WH Auden and the Irish firebrand, Dylan Thomas. Dylan had written a greatly acclaimed short poem, dedicated to his father, titled 'Do not go gentle into the good night/rage, rage against the dying of the light.' Khushwant liked it very much and was inspired to write his own essay, titled, 'Ungentle Into The Good Night.' There were other articles also that he wrote, some of them were published in the UK and Canada, but all his writing at that time was part of the life of a dilettante still wrestling with professional and sexual misadventures. He has written frankly about both, for they became, like everything else, stories to be written about in the later part of his life.

After this, Khushwant and his lovely wife socialised with

a group of lawyers, bureaucrats and officials and, once again, life drew him towards storytelling. They were all intelligent women and men of the world, and somehow they started enjoying their evenings together, when some or most of them would write down small anecdotes or stories, even jokes, and read it aloud to the group. It used to be part of a regular evening entertainment, such as cannot be imagined in the today's world of the television and other digital distractions. So, it was at that period of time when Khushwant, the bored and despairing lawyer, began writing anecdotes and little stories to read out among a group of his friends, over his beloved Scotch. It was just a social activity where people with no real literary pretensions just got together to pass their evenings by telling one another anecdotes and stories. But Khushwant found that, as he wrote those small sketches about people and read them out at those social gatherings, people would listen to him with great interest and also hang on to his every word. It was the first time when he realised that he could tell stories. An innocuous event, but it became a turning point in his life!

His love for stories about real people and their lives also took him to the most unlikely places. Though he did not care much for the business of practicing law and disliked the burdensome courtrooms, Khushwant developed a strange interest towards storytelling. At times, he would leave his work and, as a visitor, attend the lower criminal courts, where there were hearings of dacoity, murder and village crime cases. He just liked to sit there and listen to the stories, and sometimes followed it up by going to the villages where they had taken place.

He did not know it then, of course, but his fate was moving along its own unseen way to direct him to his calling and the greater purpose of his life. It was taking its time in coming but the gift was coming to Khushwant–the gift of a magnificent talent of storytelling and being able to communicate his ideas. The stories were not just fiction, for they were rooted in life. And like all storytellers in all the ages, the myth makers and shamans and priests, who could transport the listener to the challenges and victories of other lives, Khushwant too found the gift. People and events, even the most cataclysmic events like India's partition in 1947, happen and pass into history but the storyteller keeps them alive.

Initially in Lahore, and later in the hill resort of Mashobra, where his father owned a villa, Khushwant turned away from the noise and the futile life, to discover his self in the silence and the mystery of nature. He found he had a natural communion with the forests and the hills, enjoyed the sounds and songs of the trees and found sanctuary in the wild abundance of life in nature. One morning, he decided to go for "a short walk". He started walking downhill from Mashobra and enjoyed it so much that he kept on walking for more than half the day. In all, he walked almost 55 miles 2, downhill thankfully, until he reached the town of Kalka, located on the foothills. That was another Khushwant, a loner who was very happy being with himself. It was a trait that was to continue all his life. In the midst of everything that happened to him, and many wonderful things did happen, he was always alone with his thoughts. He observed his surroundings all the time and, in the midst of laughter and jesting, he was always aware.

Train to Pakistan

Khushwant wrote *Train to Pakistan* in 1954, when he was about 40 years old. With nothing much happening in his life otherwise at the time, he became a recluse for nearly three months and wrote page after page of his debut novel, reliving his experiences and observations of the events related to India's partition, which he had seen from both sides of the new border. Once he had finished his novel, it was typed by a friendly American diplomat's wife in Delhi. The lady did not think much of the novel at that time and told him so. Khushwant would have certainly been disappointed, but he still went ahead and sent the manuscript to publishers in England and America. The *Grove Press* in New York published the novel and it was well received almost everywhere.

Strangely, as we are told, that at that time in the 50s in India, writing of books was not considered as a real profession and, therefore, the writers were not considered as truly professional people. Literary pursuits were expected to be dabbled in by the cultured gentlemen, but definitely not something that men of status should be doing. This is mentioned only as an oddity of the times. Although Khushwant's novel, his first and perhaps his best, was widely appreciated, there were people who thought he was just wasting his time. However, the novel changed his life. Khushwant was now firmly on his way. His lifelong romance with the world of words had now indeed begun.

The novel reflected his own anguish and empathy with the suffering and trauma of people caught up in an aberration of history. His thinking on religious fanaticism, the politics of hate and violence, and his deep understanding of life's tragedy are reflected in a number of memorable passages from the novel. He wrote with sharp sarcasm about religion in the subcontinent. 'India is constipated with a lot of humbug. Take religion. For the Hindu, it means little besides caste and cow protection. For the Muslim, circumcision and halal meat. For the Sikh, long hair and hatred of the Muslims. For the Christian, Hinduism with a sola topee. For the Parsi, fire worship and feeding dead human bodies to vultures. Ethics, which should be the kernel of a religious code, has been carefully removed.'

About the writing of his novel, he said: 'Nothing comes naturally and everything I was doing at that time had to be learnt and worked for.' Working hard was something that he did all his life and when youngsters asked him about talent and the gift of writing, he often told them that talent was all very well but, 'you have to slog day in and day out. You can be a good journalist or a writer, but you have to slog as hard as me.' The story of the novel had been in his mind for many years and some of the characters had come from his own life. The dacoits and policeman and the doughty, pompous magistrate of the novel, Hukam Chand, was typical of the Indian administrators of that chaotic time.

He wrote painstakingly in long hand all his life. And, when in exhaustion, he stumbled with his ideas and his confidence; he went for long walks around the lake in front of his villa. The walks and the outdoors always seemed to restore a balance in him and his mind carved a connection with the nature. Not surprisingly, Jugga, the bad man of the village, is the real hero of Khushwant's novel. The fact that a devil-may-care, anti-establishment and a criminal character is shown to be capable of showing love and loyalty, and even self-sacrifice, reflects the writer's conviction that the good and the hypocritical, the so-called pillars of society (for instance, the magistrate) are most often the first to compromise and give up on human values. They are the 'humbugs' that Khushwant detested and opposed. In the novel, even as the doomed train carried hundreds of people, including Jugga's Muslim lady love, to what could be a violent death, Jugga died in a desperate bid to save them. On the other hand, the magistrate, who gave in helplessly to the forces of hatred and could do nothing to stop the massacre, lamented his own weakness, for he had to save himself.

This was to be his way of thinking all his life. A man, who was essentially free in every way, refused to follow any stereotype group thinking. It was this sense of strong and rebellious individuality which endeared him to the vast number of readers. Though people smirked and criticised his frank sexuality, they still loved it and nothing proved this more than the great popularity of *The Illustrated Weekly*, which he edited. He unabashedly published explicit text and pictures, which the traditionalists seem to lap up, even though they made a song and dance about how shocking it was. In an article in the weekly, on family planning, there was a lot of explicit talk about condoms and family planning techniques. An irate reader wrote a rather rude letter to Khushwant. 'If your respected parents had used some of these family planning methods,' wrote the reader, 'then we would not have had you among us and would not have to read such rubbish.' It was characteristic of Khushwant that he did not mind, had a good laugh and published the letter in the magazine.

It was a strong sense of the absurd that in life and his thinking made him impervious to criticism or to righteous indignation. It was essentially an understanding of the shallowness of the endemic Indian hypocrisy and his best criticism of it was to laugh it away. Like most highly intelligent people, who have also harvested life's wisdom on their journey, Khushwant had a very strong sense of the absurd. The jesting and the bluster, the 'I care a damn' attitude was an aspect not only of his natural verve, it was a part of his intellectual bravery that drove him to say it as it was.

Seriousness and wisdom do not preclude the ability to see the absurdity of the pomp and piousness that burden our lives. In fact, it is impossible to have any wisdom or understanding unless one can drop the self-importance and small minded pride that limits our thinking. Khushwant could see the absurdities of pretence and hypocrisy that are so much a part of the Indian life. It was a gift of the intellectual freedom that was part of his makeup. There was a lot of humbug in Indian religious attitudes, even more of it in Indian sexual ways and, as a writer and witness, he fought this all the time.

As much as he was a man of reflection and empathy for all human life, he was also gifted with a playfulness that accepted the darkness and tragedies of life. Perhaps that was why he saw no contradiction in the diversity of genres that he dabbled in with equal ease. He was dead serious about his facts, his research and his ideas and yet he refused to be pompous about himself. 'And we should consider that day is lost in—which we have not danced at least once. And we should call every truth false, which was not accompanied by at least one laugh,' wrote Neitzsche[1], the philosopher, who endeavoured to seek and speak the truths of life. That is perhaps also why Khushwant, always ready for a jest in his personal and social life, became so enthusiastic about joke books. He wrote once, 'It does not take much to be regarded as a humourist in a nation as humourless as ours. It is no surprise to me that my joke books have sold more than any other of my writings and that the first item most readers of my column look at is the last one that I usually put in for a joke or a humorous anecdote. I find it funny that joke books are bestsellers in a country without a sense of humour.'

All the criticism that a serious writer should not be producing, of all things the joke books, did not worry him at all. During an interview in the 80s, for the *Statesman*'s Sunday Magazine, he said, rather innocently, 'I have never really seen what the problem is. I write what I please and according to my mood. I don't think anyone lives only in one compartment. If they do, they must be very big bores. The joke books are very popular and I have enjoyed doing them. That is the only thing that counts. Indians love jokes,

---

[1]Friedrich Nietzsche (1844–1900) was a German philosopher and cultural critic. He published intensively in the 1870s and 1880s.

especially if they are dirty jokes, but it is also our habit to hide and be hypocritical.'

He wrote his columns and his books, apart from his seminal work on the history of the Sikhs. He also wrote short stories and novels and, though he felt strongly that a writer must not be trapped in a genre, the great variety of writing certainly did impact his work as a writer of pure fiction.

He wrote his novel *Delhi* in the last years of his life and, though it was promoted as a 'sprawling, Rabellesian novel', it received a lukewarm reception. It was something he never got over. It was an ambitious tribute to Delhi, a city that he loved. The book was written with much scholarship of the culture and poetry of the historic city. But it did not work. He had put his heart and soul into the novel, as it was something he had to do. He wrote, 'That's Delhi, and when life gets too much from you, all you need to do is to spend an hour at Nigambodh Ghat (a cremation ground), watch the dead being put to flames and hear their relatives wail for them. Then, come home and down a couple of pegs of whiskey. In Delhi, death and drink make life worth living.' He was in his 80s when he wrote the novel.

He wrote many other books after that but, certainly, the fire was now in its embers. It was the publishers, admirers and the socialites to whom he played sugar daddy in his last years, who egged him on to produce more books. Otherwise, we might have had less number of books and more reflective work from him. Imagine a man in his 90s, rising at five in the morning and sitting down sprawled on an old sofa, his legs up on a cane *moodha,* writing for most of the morning. 'Reading and writing is all that I have done in my life,' he has written.

Many years before the publication of *Delhi*, we had spoken to the writer Nirad C Chaudhary during an interview on Indian writers. Nirad babu was a friend of Khushwant way back in the 70s and they used to meet once in a while.

Talking about writers, writing in English, Nirad had said: 'Khushwant is first and last a storyteller, and his novels and short stories are palpably real. But he has strayed, and very successfully, into journalism. He enjoys himself there. The writer has to be a very lonely person and I happen to know that he has often called himself a loner. But I think he is too full of life to stay a loner for long.'

Indeed the double life of Khushwant continued in his alternating from creative aloofness to extensive socializing. He tried often, as recorded in his memoirs, to keep people away, to go to his villa at Kasauli and write in seclusion.But when the socialites, media, and applause came, he enjoyed it. He enjoyed the celebrity and the prominence. Many literary people have expressed their view that the quality of his writing in fiction suffered because he gave so much time to journalism and the vastly popular columns.

A street-side story with the writer

The stories were never very far from Khushwant. He observed and felt the stories played out themselves everywhere. I (Vijay Narain Shankar) was in Bombay, for it was Bombay then in 1975, when he was the editor at *Illustrated Weekly of India*. I was the editor of Sanjay and Maneka Gandhi's project—*Surya* magazine, and Khushwant was one of my advisers. The other adviser was the *Times of India* editor, Dileep Padgaonkar.

I met Khushwant often at that time, as both the editors were to be midwives at the birth of the magazine. After a drink at Khushwant's flat, just off the Gateway of India, we had a Chinese dinner at his nondescript but favourite eatery. It was getting to be 11 pm and he walked me back to my hotel. On the way, I wanted to stop for a paan. As we stood there, we noticed a dark young woman squatting on the ground and playing with her girl child. A Fiat taxi stopped in front of her. She tried to go behind the shop with her infant girl. But the taxi driver, a well-built aggressive man, shouted in Marathi to the shifty eyed *paanwallah*. There was an exchange of abuses between them. After that, the woman handed her child over to a girl in her teens and boarded the taxi.

I looked at Khushwant who had been following everything just as I had. There was an unmistakable deep sadness in his eyes. "Well," he said, with a deep sigh, 'there was not much to say. The *paanwallah* is a pimp. This happens every day. Not just here, but at a hundred places in the city. An old and never ending story!'

We walked on the parapet of the Gateway. The sea shone in the moonlight and the surf was restless, as it bounced on the rocks. He became unusually quiet after that paan shop incident. We stood there for some time but his conversation had dried up. And then he had to go. I watched him and was surprised to discover that an incident like that could sadden him so much. I had not known at that time that a writer like Khushwant could be consumed with every story of life that he saw.

The importance of being Khushwant

Living in many worlds...

When you look back upon the popularity and the importance of a man like Khushwant, you must not just look at his achievements and career milestones. There are other things, such as personality traits, nuances of attitudes and an individualistic worldview, that make up a personality. The writings and the books were his special gift, as also his gift to the world, but there was much more than that. His understanding of human nature and their stories, his irrepressible and often bawdy sense of humour and, at all times, his reflective inner seriousness set him apart from many writers. 'A writer must also live a life worth writing about,' said Ernest Hemingway once.

Khushwant, like many other great writers, went out and met life halfway; he enjoyed people, and tried to see them through the dusty mirror images. Most importantly, he was not judging them all the time. Our judgemental view distorts the ways in which we look at people. He saw them as they were.

In his lifetime, and after his passing to the happy hunting grounds, Khushwant was an icon and a celebrity. Strangely, his popularity was among two widely different kinds of people. The first group comprised his genuine readers and admirers, the educated smart set, professionals and book lovers and book launch regulars. The other was a much larger group of readers of his joke books and many followers of his sexually explicit and risqué humour. Those in the first group, or at least some of them, had read his works and celebrated an outspoken, wise and unpredictable writer. Those in the second had probably read nothing of his writings except his jokes at the end of his columns and in his joke books. Nevertheless, they all thought he was great and India's most notable writer. He was certainly the most popular in his time. His importance came from an aggressive whimsicality, from doing and saying and even writing what he wanted; and his proximity, as much as his defiance, to politicians. He was indomitable because of the freedom of his mind. A man who could live with criticism and controversy, but was never defeated.

Saying no to the ordinary

Many are the gifts of nature and qualities that drive extraordinary men to their purposes. But the one that is evident in all, and one that Khushwant had in full measure, was to never bow down and accept the ordinary. A strong self-belief overcomes external obstacles, but any self-doubt weakens a person from the within. Khushwant spent the best part of his youth drifting from one thing to another.The strongest theme of his character was non-acceptance of what he thought was wrong or unlikeable. He did not just give in and settle for a comfortable life. Lack of purpose, and meaning in what he was doing, bored him very quickly even in sinecure jobs where other men would have loved to be for lifetimes of living in the pink.

Khushwant had jobs at the Indian High Commission in London and Toronto; a plum assignment with UNESCO in Paris; an easy going job with All India Radio (AIR) ; and a journalistic stint with the government's *Yojana* magazine. After sticking on for brief periods, he resigned from all these jobs because (a) he defied haughty men, such as his Indian High Commission boss, VK Krishna Menon; (b) got bored at UNESCO and at AIR; and (c) disliked being a bureaucrat at *Yojana*. This was doubtless the restlessness of a man who had a destiny but did not yet know what it was.

Cutting Krishna Menon to size

Krishna Menon, the Indian High Commissioner in London, was Khushwant's boss and, as things turned out, it was a perpetual slanging match, full of sound and fury from Menon and a deep dislike on the part of Khushwant.

Khushwant's first meeting with Menon was a disaster, as the latter was known to be rather short tempered and rude. That set the tone for the days and months that were to follow and Khushwant just would not take the man's crotchety temper, bad behaviour and imperious ways. Khushwant wrote, 'A friend assured me that Krishna Menon was the finest brain he had ever met and compared favourably with Stalin (who was not known to be a particularly fine brain)... Menon was the most unpredictable and complex character I had ever met.'

He shared the story of Menon's tantrums with his staff, the short tempered and crude behaviour and his constant sparring and picking faults with whatever Khushwant did. In London, Khushwant was responsible for seeing to it that the London newspaper carried only the stories that were pro-India and he was found wanting at many times. Once, when Jawaharlal Nehru was in London, a private dinner was arranged at a little-known Greek restaurant for Lady Mountbatten and Nehru. There was not much security those days and the dinner was supposed to be a quiet affair between the Indian Prime Minister and Lady Mountbatten;

their affair being part of the Indian history. However, the restaurant owner recognised the two and informed the Press. The next morning's papers carried pictures and stories of Lady Mountbatten and Nehru sitting close to each other in deep conversation. There was a great furore at India House and Menon was livid.

Khushwant was told that Jawaharlal Nehru wanted to see him. When he went to Claridges Hotel London, where Nehru was staying, Khushwant was directed towards the sitting room of the Indian Prime Minister. He was justifiably nervous and approached Nehru, who did not seem to understand why he was there.

'You asked to see me, Sir,' Khushwant presented himself.

'Did I? Who are you?' Nehru asked, with surprise.

'I am the press attaché in charge of publicity,' Khushwant introduced himself.

Nehru looked at him and finally decided to end the interview with some pointed sarcasm,' 'You have a strange idea of publicity.'

It was a mild reprimand, but a reprimand nevertheless, from Jawaharlal Nehru whom the world was watching closely and especially his own countrymen, for stories of his affair with Lady Mountbatten had been rife for a long time. Khushwant was deflated though it was none of his fault.

Though the meeting ended with a gentle remark by Nehru, the relationship between Lady Mountbatten and the

Indian Prime Minister had always been a sensitive issue, and the publicity it had received in London made Menon even angrier with him. Soon after that incident, Khushwant, tired of the routine, the constant unpleasantness with Menon, and the pointlessness of his life, resigned and decided to return to India, with thoughts of writing seriously. Later, in London, he shared a flat with a lady who worked at India House for some time.

Menon, for all his faults and his frugal life of a miser, had a glad eye for pretty women and the stories of his affairs with the India House staff were common. 'The last time I spoke to Menon,' recounted Khushwant, 'was on the telephone. I happened to be in London working at the India House library. I was sharing a flat with Sheila Lall. We had a common telephone. Every night she was out with one of her many lovers. The telephone rang, but when I picked it up and said "hello", it went dead. I complained to Sheila, "That must be Krishna!"'

She told me, 'He wants me to be his mistress, with no strings attached.' The next time the telephone rang, instead of saying the customary 'hello', I spat out with anger, 'you bloody bastard, I know who you are. Stop ringing at this hour or you will hear worse.' There were no more calls after that.'

He was never one to take nonsense of any kind and that remained a trait all his life. In fact, it became a trademark of his writing and also a reason for his popularity. People who read him, or looked for, found his intolerance against sham and stupidity. His fearlessness endeared him to people who, more often than not, were quite used to living with all kinds of fear, of gods, of bosses and rulers, and of social taboos. That certainly was one of the things that made him special.

A leap in the dark

While in London, and tired of the India House job, Khushwant made his first forays into writing. He had been writing off and on and just when his relations with Menon were becoming too much for him, a collection of his short stories, *The Mark of Vishnu and Other Stories,* based on his days as a lawyer in Lahore, was published. Though it did not sell very well, it got excellent reviews and he had to be content with that. He was left with two hundred unsold copies that had to be stacked up in his room. Quite a number of those stories were published by *The Illustrated Weekly* of India and Khushwant was very happy with that. 'I had other books brewing inside me… I had enough money to last me six months in England.'

He decided to resign from his job. It was entirely a leap in the dark for a man who had become accustomed to the good life as he had always lived well. It is impossible to say what was going on in his mind at the time, but one can well imagine that a certain restless angst drove him away from the safety and security of what he had. And, as usual, what also drove him away was his sense of purposelessness in his life and the job that he felt he was trapped in. One way or another, money had not been a dire problem for Khushwant. What he experienced was the sense of boredom with life and the fear that this may continue endlessly.

He was not exactly a young man and had a family to look after. The skills for which he had been trained were of no use to him now. So he settled down in a small cottage, sent his family home, and got down to the adventure of a new beginning. He did an English translation of the Sikh scripture, the *Japji Sahib*. It was just like Khushwant and a mark of his obstinate self-belief, that being neither a scholar of the scripture of his religion, nor even knowing the Punjabi Gurmukhi script very well, he used translation dictionaries and completed the job. A friend who knew a publisher got it printed. He was happy with his work and it was the beginning of his lasting interest in working on subjects that were concerned with Sikhism.

Shooting off his opinions

Khushwant decided quite astutely that, if he was to write with any success, he must do the unusual and use his Sikh background and write about things that were not commonly written about. He then penned *A Short History of the Sikhs*. It was a hastily done job of no great merit, which he admitted. However, being the first book of its kind on the subject, it was widely reviewed in the British press. It was also a work that created quite a storm. In this hastily done history, he did a Khushwant and shot off an opinion that was outrageous and angered many in the Sikh community.

'I added my own prophecy that, if the pace at which young Sikhs were beginning to give up emblems of the Khalsa faith (unshorn hair and beards) continued, the Khalsa form of Sikhism would disappear by the turn of the century and the Sikhs, like the Jains and Buddhists, would relapse into the mainstream of Hinduism.' It was an outrageous statement by a person who had nothing but a nodding acquaintance with Sikhism. This created quite a furore in orthodox Sikh circles in India. Controversy became his regular bedfellow in his later years too and his columns thrived on it. Certainly, it gave him a great sense of prominence.

Outspoken to a fault, he was forever in a truth or dare frame of mind. When the entire world panned the declaration of Emergency in India and Sanjay Gandhi, Khushwant supported both but later regretted. Indeed his opinions were often hasty and very unpopular but he seemed not to care and usually stood by them until such time as he himself began to feel that a change of heart was necessary.

He was a stubborn man and remained so to the last days of his life-stubborn in his opinions, even when they were faulted, and stubborn about giving his opinion about things that he should probably have stayed away from. This was certainly true about politics and his opinions about people in politics. And yet, such was the mystique and the popular acceptance that he had created about himself, that even his most controversial opinions were lapped up by people, discussed as the words of a crazy savant and picked up by the media. He was stubborn about his writing too. Even when he was just one year short of the Vedic lifespan of a hundred, Khushwant, with a frail body, had a sharp mind and never gave up writing to the end. It was the sacred ritual of his life.

A writer as a celebrity

During his lifetime, Khushwant became a celebrity and icon. He was adopted by the smart set, the politically savvy liberals and the illuminati of Delhi. They loved his risqué jesting, his impatience with hypocrisy and the hint of greatness in his shocking pronouncements that sounded very close to the truth, his openness and plain common sense values. Certainly, there was greatness in his pragmatic wisdom, his no nonsense approach to sex, religion and the business of living, which had all been complicated by taboos and irrational thinking. But when a writer gets a rock star fan following, not so much for his books, but for his *shock and snob* values, then he is watched closely because the media takes a cue from his fan following and builds him up for all the wrong reasons.

Indeed the Khushwant celebration at elegant literary

soirees, book launches and his private Khushwant Litfest had been unprecedented. No other Indian writer has had this kind of adulation heaped upon him. More power, of course, came to this extraordinary man, but all of this deflected his formidable creative powers towards popular, or shall we say populist writing? He had observed that his joke books outsold all his other writings. He had built up a readership that would never get near his serious works. As far as Khushwant was concerned, it did not seem to bother him what was populist and what was profound. He just happened to enjoy writing, to shoot off his opinions about everything and his each book was a frame for a tremendously lively mind that was involved in everything. 'We do not write because we want to,' said one of Khushwant's favourite writers, W. Somerset Maugham, 'we write because we have to.' This was most certainly true about Khushwant, for he dipped his persistent pen into every event, opinion, controversy and discussion that moved the minds of people. Perhaps, that was the reason why so many people hung on to his every word.

A visit by President Kalam

The writing was his very life and he wrote every day of his day, right to his last days. He was frail and weak in his 99th year, but as his writer son, Rahul Singh, says, 'his mind was clear.' In the extraordinary importance that Khushwant achieved, there were also other contributing factors. His prominence in the intellectual life of the nation, as also his falling in and falling out with the Gandhi family; the Padma Bhushan award that he returned in 1984 to protest against the army action at the Golden Temple at Amritsar; and the higher Padma Vibhushan award that he received in 2011, were all parts of an extraordinary life. He was unwell and was told that the President of India wanted to come over and see him at his house. Khushwant did not believe it first, for although he had received much acclaim and honour in his life, it was totally unprecedented that the President would actually visit him at his house. Only when the security people arrived to sanitize the area, did the *Old Warrior of the Pen* finally believe it.

President Kalam had written a highly inspiring and idealistic book, *On Wings of Fire*, as his offering to ignite young minds and Khushwant had not given it a good review. He thought of that as President Kalam arrived at his door, but that never came up. President Kalam was gracious and friendly, as he had come to honour a great Indian writer. He looked at the row of books in Khushwant's house while exchanging pleasantries. There was a large crowd of people outside the house, as the word had spread that the President had come to see the writer. Khushwant had been persuaded to wear some nice clothes, as he normally prided himself on being the 'worst dressed man in India'. Khushwant talked mainly about books and was visibly pleased to see President

Kalam. Other national leaders, including Mrs Indira Gandhi and Sanjay Gandhi, had also come to see him at his house at different times in the past. When Rajeev Gandhi visited Khushwant at his residence, he got a taste of the writer's fad about time. As related by Rahul singh, 'My dad made a very moving speech after dinner. He said that every member of the Gandhi family had been to his house, including Rajeev's mother and brother. He was happy that Rajeev could make it for the first time and said he felt honoured. Then surprisingly added, 'however it's time for me to go to bed. Good night,' and then left.'

It is rare to find instances of prime ministers and presidents of a country visiting writers at their houses. In diplomatic circles, there was a perception that Khushwant, though being a Rajya Sabha member and close to political leaders, was also one of the few intellectuals who understood the Indian scene better than others. It became an almost mandatory ritual for new ambassadors and diplomats to visit him, on their arrival in India, to get his point of view on the situation in the country. I used to work for the German news at the West German embassy and the following story was told by the press counsellor, Thomas Mattusek, who had accompanied the German ambassador to Khushwant's house for dinner. After dinner, the ambassador had pulled out a cigar for an after-meal smoke. But he was told politely that he would enjoy his cigar more in his car. He was also told that it was time for Khushwant to go to bed.

Indeed the legend of Khushwant grew in a myriad of ways. It was more than his writing, of course. It was all the things that he was; his odd uncaring sense of doing and saying what he thought was right. Generally, most people live quiet lives of conformity, though they also yearn to break free in the ways they think and live their lives. A man like Khushwant surprised them with his everyday bravery of ideas and absence of fearing the consequences.

There was an even chance that he was conscious of his odd ball persona. He knew he raised eyebrows with his off-colour stories and endless jokes collected from fans and everyone he talked to, which included street tea stall regulars, working people, drivers and drinking cronies. When his detractors abused him and sent him hate mail with abuses, he laughed and printed the abuses in the magazines he edited. His huge sense of fun was the secret of his indestructibility.

Of course, he knew he was notorious and enjoyed it immensely. Interestingly, he knew exactly where and with whom he could be notorious. Speaking at the Khushwant Singh Litfest in Kasauli last year, Ameena Sayyid, Managing Director of Oxford University Press in Pakistan, said, the writer was one of her favourite persons. She recalled her first meeting with Khushwant in Delhi, in 1980, at his house. 'I was awestruck,' she told a gathering of Khushwant admirers at the Litfest, 'by this man who cracked a dirty joke about a donkey, which I cannot recount here.' He did not offend and could get away with anything.

Whiskey and urine therapy

It would be quite a list, if it was ever made, of the things that Khushwant could get away with. If it was jokes, the dirtier, the better; and he recounted them with a most innocent face and a tentative smile. Yet he did not seem to offend, even if he told his juiciest jokes to elegant ladies. He was too intelligent to offend. And in his armoury of shock values he had all sorts of surprise statements. He had almost made a career out of them. Sometimes, it would appear that he got into an opinion–a frame of mind–out of his conviction, but then held himself in spite of criticism and clear evidence that he was wrong. Perhaps, that was an aspect of his stubbornness. Or perhaps, he enjoyed walking out of line.

Much of this does apply perfectly to his obsessive support for Sanjay Gandhi, which he never lived down. Anyway, it certainly got him into all kinds of trouble. Morarji Desai had become the Prime Minister of India, after defeating Indira Gandhi, following the Emergency. Khushwant was the editor of *The Illustrated Weekly*. He had undertaken a survey on the popularity of leaders, in which readers cast their votes. As it turned out, Sanjay Gandhi, the enfant terrible of the Emergency, was declared the winner and the most popular leader in India.

The survey was the worst possible thing to have been undertaken at a time when there was an anti-Mrs Gandhi and anti-Sanjay wave in the country and when Morarji, a man bitterly opposed to Indira, was the Prime Minister. But Khushwant, probably driven by his loyalty to a fallen friend, had published the survey and drew heavy flak from all sides. Morarji made a visit to Mumbai (then Bombay) and Khushwant met him at the airport. The Prime Minister was seemingly angry with Khushwant and made it quite plain to him. He also complained that the survey had been rigged, but agreed to give him an interview. As things turned out, Khushwant had probably gone too far with his support to Sanjay and, as a result, was soon given marching orders from the editorship of the weekly. It was a sharp price to pay. Khushwant also found later, much to his dismay, that the survey had indeed been rigged. A number of readers, perhaps prompted by interested parties, had cast hundreds of bogus votes, supporting Sanjay.

Khushwant was too important an editor for Morarji to ignore. He was called for an interview with the Prime Minister. During the interview, Khushwant asked all sorts of questions about the Emergency and its aftermath, as well as Morarji's plans to impose prohibition in the country. Quite obviously, Khushwant was particularly interested in the matter of prohibition. Morarji confirmed that he certainly would impose prohibition.

Those were the days when many states had prohibition and dry days. On dry days, Indians were not allowed to drink alcohol, whereas if you had a foreign passport you could drink at a five-star hotel. This led to a particularly ridiculous situation in which, if you were an Indian entertaining a foreigner, you usually ordered a whiskey for the foreigner and a Coke for yourself. Then both you and your guest shared the whiskey, drinking it alternately and left Coke for the waiter.

At the interview, the Prime Minister asked Khushwant to switch off the tape, as he wanted to have a man-to-man chat. 'You make fun of my insistence on prohibition and advocating urine therapy,' said Morarji, 'if I persuade you that drinking is bad for you, will you give it up?'

'I have been drinking for forty years,' said Khushwant. 'I have never been drunk even once in my life. If I persuade you that drinking is not bad for you, will you have a drink?' he asked in reply.

'He thought over my suggestion for a while,' Khushwant later recounted', and then replied, 'It is a fair offer; if you persuade me that drinking alcohol is not bad for health, I promise to try it."'

Having made such headway with the man of many fads, Khushwant was not one to stand down. He next asked Morarji about his insistence on abstinence from sex. 'I do not want to discuss that subject with you,' said the Prime Minister, probably giving the 'dirty old man' a dirty look. The interview was over.

The offer of whiskey to the teetotaller Morarji a man obsessed with abstinence and bringing prohibition all over India, was a preposterous one. Even for Khushwant. Morarji had made a name for himself all over the world as a drinker of his own urine. He followed an ancient Indian medicinal practice, called Shivambhookalp, in which a person drinks his own urine first thing in the morning. It was also a practice developed in the century, as an alternative medicine in the UK by a Dr Armstrong, known as Auto Urine Therapy. Morarji made no bones about it and spoke like an evangelist whenever he went about the benefits of drinking urine, one of which was longevity. As it happened, however, Morarji and the inveterate whiskey drinker, Khushwant, both lived to the magic age of 99 years. Khushwant, most decidedly, would have enjoyed his stint much more.

A mentor and an icon

It was a life in many worlds, lived by a man who could just not have enough of it with all its varied experiences. A rollercoaster of a ride of exploration of people and ideas, finding out the stories that men live and leave behind them, and never ever stagnating in the safety of what was accepted or popular. The young, especially the journalists and writers, flocked to meet him and he never disappointed them, perhaps because he remembered his own struggle and his initial self-doubts as a writer.

'He was an invaluable mentor or... a scholar and a much revered icon of the Sikhs,' writes Suneet Vir Singh, a freelance writer. Khushwant was her guide and mentor. She began her career by writing a biography of Guru Gobind Singh, which she co-authored with Khushwant. She then worked as a television producer with Doordarshan. She also wrote in numerous publications on women's issues. She edited and published a fortnightly digest of the regional press in India, titled India Speaks. She is married to Mani Shankar Aiyar, former diplomat and now a member of the Congress party.

Suneet Vir Singh,writes; 'Marriages are like watermelons; in every hundred, you will find one good one', so goes a Spanish saying. H.G. Wells juggled three mistresses and, at any given time, simultaneously cheated on them. Bertrand Russell married for the fourth time when he was 80. Somerset Maugham turned gay in his 70s. 'Sex appeal lies in the wallet of her beholder', writes Sobha De. These gems and many more are all documented in his book Khushwant Singh on Women, Sex, Love and Lust, an anthology of the Sardar in the Bulb's writings on some of his favourite subjects.Reading the pieces compiled in this book, one learns a great deal about Urdu poetry, John Donne's poems, Sufi mystics, love and life in New York, Acharya Rajneesh's salvation through sex... but what about Khushwant himself? Khushwant was far from being a dirty old man; he was neither a drunkard nor a lecherous womaniser. I knew him as my friend Rahul's father, as an invaluable mentor, as a writer and a scholar, as a much revered icon of the Sikhs and, in later years, as an uncle whose fund of limitless humour, scholarship and acerbic commentary on life and times in India today made the gin and tonic quite superfluous.

Forever ready to listen, joke and make you laugh at the crazy world that we live in, I never once saw him drunk, nor have I encountered any woman who claims that he made a pass at her! He was full of warmth and empathy for anyone who rang his doorbell though always 'only by prior appointment', as the notice on the entrance door to Flat No. 49-E proclaimed.

Khushwant's passion for writing dictated a strict daily regime, which he refused to compromise, come what may. Drink at 7 pm, dinner at 8 pm and bed by 9 pm up every morning at the crack of dawn to write for several hours at a stretch. No one, no matter how powerful, glamorous or rich and famous may be, could make him deviate from his time table. When he moved to Mumbai as the editor of *The Weekly*, he was besieged by invitations from publicity hungry Bollywood stars and politicians. But the glitterati did not impress him. Whether it was a birthday bash of Nargis or the Chief Minister's banquet, Khushwant would head home well before dinner was served.

What was his USP ? I am convinced that Khushwant was an old fashioned romantic at heart. He revealed the truth about himself in a piece titled 'The Language of Love'. Describing his theory of love, he wrote:

'The basic cause which makes us seek the love of another person is because we are extremely lonely. Gertrude Stein called this void inner loneliness. I prefer to describe it as the inner solitude – the feeling of being all alone in the world. At times we feel this solitude with greater poignancy and it is almost like physical pain. It can come upon us suddenly and without warning – as in the early hours of the morning. It can be brought on by the wail of a locomotive as it speeds through the black of the night not knowing where it has come from or where it is going; it may be brought on by the sight of a heron – just one – in a vast sky at dusk. This inner solitude is something of a paradox. At any time it is like an aching void begging to be filled by the warmth of affection of another; at others it becomes a walled fortress with a notice bearing the warning: 'Keep out'.'

It was his weekly column in the *Hindustan Times* 'With Malice towards One and All, which made Khushwant a household name. What won him an all India fan club was the simplicity and candour with which he wrote about day-to-day happenings, about our lives!

In his later years, the theme was about the travails of passing from the middle years into old age; the nuisance of constipation, the pain of the final farewell to loved ones, the warmth of being with old friends, the never failing glow lighting the soul after that first sip of Scotch at 7 pm sharp, the thrill of re-reading Ghalib…

And what about his success with women? Why did writers, dancers, singers, politicians, women from every walk of life, from Nargis to Maneka Gandhi, flock to his drawing room at 7 pm, only to be thrown out at 8 pm sharp always.

Even his most ardent female admirers would not describe him as tall and handsome. He had no sex appeal – at least I did not think so. He was not in the habit of throwing diamond bracelets at damsels at his soirees. The answer lied in his sincere respect for the women, as human beings, equal to the men, and not as inferior creatures to be enslaved or used by men and society. He was a diehard feminist, as depicted in his following writing:

'The fact is, men have abused women from the day Eve was born out of Adam's rib. They have created myths about their being low on intelligence, poor in physique, devious in their ways and totally unreliable, and repeated their ad nauseam for so long that most women accepted them to be true and developed an inferiority complex. It was only in the last century that women began to question assumptions of male superiority, claimed equal rights and hit back with vigour at their denigrators as male chauvinist pigs. While men have conceded that women are every bit as good as anyone in all fields of activity, women have not forgiven them for the centuries of humiliation they had to suffer and constantly remind them of their past misdeeds'.

Three cheers for Khushwant who fearlessly wrote what he thought and never searched for a condom for his pen. As there was more laughter than malice in his heart, to end this little remembrance, the following is one of his classic Santa-Banta jokes:

'Santa was flying to Chandigarh from Pune. He was allotted a middle seat but decided to take the window seat instead, which had been allotted to an old lady. The lady requested Santa to exchange the seats and let her sit on the seat allotted to her. He refused, saying, "I want to see the view from the window." The old lady complained to the air hostess who requested Santa to sit on his allotted middle seat. Santa was adamant and bluntly refused. The air hostess went up to the co-pilot. He too came and requested Santa, but in vain. Finally, the captain of the aircraft came. He whispered something in Santa's ears. Santa immediately vacated the window seat and took the middle seat. Astonished, the air hostess and the co-pilot asked the captain what he had said to Santa. The captain replied: "Nothing, I just told him that only the middle seats will go to Chandigarh. All others were going to Jalandhar."

The iconoclast Chacha K

Important as he was in high places, Khushwant was special to everyone in the family. Geetanjali Singh Chandra, the writer's niece, talks of a well-loved uncle who was always involved with his books. Speaking at the Khushwant Singh LitFest 2016 at Kasauli, she spoke warmly of some of the things that made him so special: 'We all, of course, know Chacha K as an iconoclast—as someone who not just crossed borders and boundaries but often tore them down. But I always think of him as "dwelling in duality". There was the Khushwant who created and projected a persona of himself as a 'dirty old man' reveling in this image and taking wicked pleasure in exaggerating these exploits. And then there was the Khushwant who awoke every morning at 4 am to work on history of the Sikhs and other writings; the cultivated image of the fun loving "Joker Man" and the reality of a hardworking author, rechecking every word written.

He claimed to be an atheist, but had mentioned that he had felt the presence of Guru Nanak while he wrote *A History of Sikhs*. He told lewd jokes and wrote about his various exploits with women, real or imagined, but his respect for women and open acknowledgement of them as equals was unshakeable. And how could it be otherwise, with his wife, Kaval; his daughter, Mala; and his granddaughter, Naina, all being strong women, who brooked no nonsense?

Whenever I came to see him, slipping in through the back door, his first words were always: 'Take a look at these books, pointing to the pile on the table, and take whatever you want.' When I received my PhD, he chuckled and congratulated me, and said, 'You are the first person in the family to have earned a doctoral degree.' And when Naina got her doctoral degree, he proudly and triumphantly announced that I was now not the only one!

In 1988, Khushwant Chacha came to Washington DC to the Smithsonian's Wilson Centre for International Scholars to update *A History of Sikhs*. My husband and I were then living there. I wormed my way into his heart because I could decipher his scrawl. He wrote everything by hand. Every day, he would hand me a sheaf of handwritten papers, his output of the day, and I would put it on the computer and bring him the printed copies. Then he would edit that (by hand) and next time I would put in the corrections and bring him a fresh set to look at. His wonderment at his increased speed and productivity was joyful.

Idly, chatting one day, he mentioned that he had this manuscript for a novel that he had written a while ago, but it was now faded and tattered, and the pages were crumpled and full of holes. He did not even know if it was worth publishing, as the pages were all over the place. I offered to straighten it out and get him a clean and strong photocopy. He demurred a bit but then gave it to me. That was his novel *Delhi*.

No matter where we went, a restaurant, a mall, or in a taxi, there was always someone who recognized him and would come up to greet him and shake his hand. Indians abroad were so proud of him. They claimed that he put both India and the Sikhs on the international map. And they wanted him to know how much they valued him. They valued him not only for his many columns, novels, short stories, translations or joke books, but mainly for being *mouphat* (outspoken) and fearlessly telling it like it was. They admired him for criticizing the high and mighty politicians and leaders, for speaking out against hypocrisy and for castigating religious leaders who encouraged people to indulge in silly rituals. But most of all, he was loved and respected for speaking and writing directly and without pretension.

Our favourite family story though was about Khushwant Chacha's dress sense, probably as a reaction to his father's very proper Saville Row suit culture. His loosely tied turban and crumpled T-shirts were a direct dare to his father. This was in spite of the oft told story of his father having sent back one of his sons to change into a suit for a family gathering that he was hosting for his brother, then the Governor of Madras (not yet Chennai). However, Khushwant Chacha had inherited his father's punctuality, if not his dress sense. Lunch and dinner at his father's house were served at fixed hours and, if you crossed the sacred hour, you were not served food. Once when my grandfather's only son-in-law arrived half an hour late for a meal; he was told in no uncertain terms that this was not a restaurant and he would have to eat elsewhere.

But the story that became a family lore was about Khushwant Chacha's visiting hours, which were from 7pm to 8 pm, regardless of who you were. Once, the then President of India, Zail Singh, who perhaps did not know this rule, had dropped in at his home to visit him. At 8.00 pm, the President of India was shown the door, as it was Khushwant Chacha's dinner time. I believe the same thing happened to then Prime Minister of India, Manmohan Singh, and his wife some years later. I know they had at least left with a smile.

His column,With Malice to all, signalled another duality -- the malicious, gossipy columnist, who sometimes had poor judgment about people and the large-hearted secularist, who welcomed people of all faiths and points of view, especially if they disagreed with him, or especially if they were good looking and from Pakistan. And the affection was mutual. The last testament to his duality is that his ashes are present both in India and Pakistan.

The wise jester

Shoba De wrote of him after he passed away: 'Khushwant had one of the liveliest, liveliest, liveliest minds I have ever known.' She had collaborated with him on a book, Uncertain Liaisons–Sex, strife and Togetherness in Urban India. It was a book, far ahead of its time, on changing attitudes to sex and romance in modern times. The collaboration was never boring, as she writes: 'Khushwant was a man firing on all cylinders at all times.'

So it was that his mind and his creative writings, like his life and restless rush to do more, to touch every event and shade of the world in which he lived, like a river that made its own way and went wherever he willed. It was a dream run for a wise man who was also an irrepressible jester.

The journalism juggernaut & The Weekly

A phenomenal success and a bitter aftertaste

Khushwant had been on the periphery of media for a long time and it seemed as if his fate was pushing him towards writing and journalism, by fits and starts. While he did a little bit of this and a little bit of that, in his early years, media seemed to be following him doggedly. After being a press attaché in London and Ottawa, and the editor of *Yojana* magazine, he had joined All India Radio, where he complained of having no work. It was his free ranging and maverick mind that drove him to take an interest in all kinds of people and events, a persistent knack of observation and the insistence on finding out the story behind everything, leading him steadily to the fourth estate. When he did get there, it was not due to any of his intention or any preparation but because he had already written a novel and also undertaken a very important work–*A History of Sikhs*. He was getting known. And the wheels were moving.

The break of a lifetime

In has been said that, in 1968, Khushwant was 'parachuted into the chair' of the editor at *The Illustrated Weekly of India*, in Bombay. Generally, most people have to start at the base level, and then slave their way up through heaps of copyediting, or through years of reporting, before they can get anywhere. Khushwant in his mid-40s had already written his novel, *Train to Pakistan*, and also had undertaken teaching assignments on Sikhism at various universities after the publication of his book, *A History of Sikhs*. His short stories had also won him a critical acclaim. Based on his works, there were offers from *The Illustrated Weekly of India*, India's only family magazine at that time, for Khushwant to take over as editor. It was a time of many great journalists and editors, such as Frank Moraes, Prem Bhatia and RK Karanjia, and journalism in India was mostly concentrated on news and daily journalism. The magazines, including the weekly, were considered as soft journalism, as they were published mainly for the family use and, therefore, concerned primarily with art and culture, contemporary literature and, only marginally, with films and sport. Up until that time, in 1968, the national English language magazines in India could be counted on the fingers of a hand. They were all a very sedate, conservative and usually an unexciting affair.

Khushwant had taken over a very old magazine and turned it upside down. The magazine was selling about sixty thousand copies a week. In a time of no television or internet, the magazine was an extension of the popular idea of family entertainment at the time, which was provided by great writers, great artists, writings on Bharatanatyam and other classical dancing, and loaded with literary short stories and articles. Khushwant changed all that in a few weeks. He was like a bull in a china shop, as he dumped age-old regular columns and profound artistic pages from the magazine. Initially bewildered, the weekly staff soon caught up with the road-roller mood of their new editor. As one of his younger writers at the time, Bachi Karkaria (nee Kanga) was to say later: 'Khushwant was far ahead of his time, as he changed the content and face of the magazine. Much of what we see now in the profusion of Indian magazines, in terms of the glitz and glamour, the controversy and the investigative features, is a development from what he did for the weekly. There were many who thought at the time that, what Khushwant was doing, was too sudden and perhaps even uncalled for.'

Some of the drastic changes in the weekly were not liked at all. There used to be a two-page spread, They Were Married, which was a presentation of wedding pictures of newly married couples from all over India. It was considered an honour, as well as a matter of pride, for people living in the big and the small towns in the country to have their pictures published in the magazine. Without much ado, he dropped it. Another feature that did not find favour with him was *Aunty Wendy's* Column. This was a popular children's page, which held Weekly competitions in essays, poetry and crafts, and gave away prizes. Well remembered by those in their early teens till the mid-60s both above columns were popular and encouraged the reader participation, but they did not fit into the Khushwant scheme of things. He was looking to break down the dullness, and bring in glamour and excitement–the worldview of the new age, where Elvis Presley, the Beatles, the new bold Hollywood films, and the first pictures of streakers at cricket matches were the order of the day.

He did the unthinkable. He introduced glamour pictures, a full page offering to the voyeur, and lost no opportunity in including innocent pictures of women, sometimes even tribal or village women, in the magazine. Perhaps one of the most controversial moves he made at that time was a full length photo feature in the magazine on a popular *quawalli* and *nazm* singer of Lucknow, Shakila Bano Bhopali, known for her provocative and risqué repartee with her audiences and her double meaning jokes, as she entertained large crowds of admirers. The controversy would seem unimportant today. At that time, however, Shakila Bano was considered a *mujra* singer, almost at the level of the singing and dancing girls of old Lucknow and was certainly not to be seen by people from decent families, leave alone the children. A Shakila Bano feature in *The Weekly*, complete with her pictures, salacious quotes, and her often inebriated admirers, did two things: it upset people and became a talking point, with expressions of righteous indignation; and it also did the opposite—it evoked interest and enjoyment, guilt and delight. That was to become the hallmark, or certainly the formula, that Khushwant was to use in the weekly and perhaps, later in his life, in much of his other popular writing.

Bachi Karkaria, now a well-known and gifted writer, with a sense of humour that is highly intelligently but crazy, joined the weekly at about the same time as Khushwant became its editor. She writes with affection and admiration for him, as he played mayhem with the magazine and took it from strength to strength. She writes: 'He had rescued the weekly from its dog-eared destination-waiting-room formula of success and taken it to unimaginable heights of popularity and influence...various people attribute the weekly's success to the salacious called "what the reader wants."'

The circulation of the magazine went from average to raving. At its highest, it had touched a figure of well over four lakh. He gave opportunities to numerous youngsters and never shut himself out. Among the many good journalists that achieved prominence later were Bachi Karkaria herself, as well as MJ Akbar, Bikram Vohra, Jiggs Kalra and Raju Bharatan.

The Weekly was one big ride to success for the new editor and Khushwant broke all the rules. He did a huge series on various communities of India. *The Weekly* presented each and every little known caste and community, with its myths and history, its great achievers and iconic men and women, and people just lapped it up. Khushwant had been successful in his estimation that people from each community would definitely want to read about themselves and their peers. Another success was a series on cricket done by the veteran journalist Raju Bharatan, which took the circulation up to its very highest of 4.60 lakh copies.

He was also befriended by a number of film personalities and film writers. Among them, he spoke much of the fiery pimpernel of film journalism, the once very famous Devyani Chaubal, who had made a career out of lampooning and tearing the characters of film stars to shreds. He was friendly with her and followed all her activities, as she got manhandled by top actors like Dharmendra and got her hair soaked in beer by the sons of a top film star.

He also found the time to go to Pakistan, where he met Begum Para, who had married the actor Dilip Kumar's brother, Nasir Khan. He spent the evening with the ageing star, during which Begum Para finished his bottle of Scotch and Khushwant nurse-maided her through her drunken mishaps, as she fell twice on the sidewalk. It was the kind of thing that he often got into, as he loved meeting people and enjoyed, or shall we say, observed, the good as well as the romance of the unusual.

Among the great stars of the time that he met was Nargis. She had asked him if she could stay at his villa at Kasauli during a brief visit. Khushwant, as usual, had to jest with the great actress when he said to her, 'Of course, you can stay at Kasauli at my place on the condition that you will give me permission to tell people that you slept in my bed.' The actress broke into peals of laughter and said, 'Done.'

Khushwant and Nargis were later nominated to the Rajya Sabha at the same time and were allocated seats next to each other. Khushwant recounted: 'When anyone tried to introduce us, Nargis would say, 'You don't have to introduce us. I have slept in his bed.'''

It was during his time at Bombay that Khushwant received a proposal by the Ivory-Merchant duo to make a film of his novel, *Train to Pakistan*. One of the top actors of that time, Shashi Kapoor, was to play the lead role and Shabana Azmi was to play the heroine. It was a great project that Khushwant supported. They hired a well-known author and writer to write the dialogues for the film; the gentleman drank up a lot of Khushwant's Scotch every evening. After some months, the project was suddenly dropped and Khushwant rued the fact that gallons of his Scotch had been consumed and his time wasted.

And Katy Mirza was there too

One of the young journalists whom Khushwant befriended during his time at the weekly was Vinod Mehta, who went on to become a highly respected editor of newspapers and magazines. Vinod must have been in his early 30s then and was the editor of a Playboy clone, a much watered-down Indian version due to austerity laws in India, a magazine called *Debonair.* This was the late 60s after all and the influences from the west in magazines and media were just trickling into India. Mehta had a difficult time trying to get women to pose in something close to the altogether, for it was unheard of that ladies from good families in India would ever do such a thing. In a conservative country, where magazines like *Playboy* were read surreptitiously by diehard voyeurs, which included family men, just discovering the freedom of sexuality, and college kids, who thought that in a world of Marilyn Monroe, swimsuit beauty contests and moon landings, it was the done thing to look at pictures of nude women.

By hook or by crook, Mehta did his job with great determination and scoured the nightclubs and dance bars and wherever else he could find women willing to disrobe, at least partially. He promptly sent his cameras and got them for his large size centre spreads. They were not as sensational as Playboy, but they would do for India at that time. He met Khushwant for an interview in 1969 and asked him what he had done during his time at London. Khushwant said,

'F—king, cheese and wine.' Mehta, never devoid of a sense of humour, used that 'wonderful sentence' of Khushwant as the title of a chapter in his book, *Bombay: A Private View*. The two men also discovered another 'bond.' This happened to be an interest in nude pinups. One of the great voluptuous pinups, who had become a *Playboy* bunny with her supposedly '48-36-46' figure, was in India for some years and had even acted in Hindi films. Her full bodied pinup spreads appeared in many magazines, as also in Mehta's *Debonair*.

Khushwant expressed a wish to meet Katy and his young friend readily arranged it. So it was that the weekly editor had a date with a top pinup model of the time, Katy Mirza, and if one is to believe Mehta, the twinkle eyed Sardar enjoyed himself having 'Scotch with Katy.'

A mentor for life

Then a young journalist, Chandni Luthra, was new to The Times of India. So it was that the budding journalist made her debut under the watchful eye of Khushwant, who selected her as a trainee journalist in the Mumbai office of the TOI, soon after he took over as editor of *The Illustrated Weekly of India*. 'There is nothing more I could have asked for', she writes. She left the weekly after some time. Later, she switched over to marketing and public relations when she joined Indian Tourism Development Corporation (ITDC). After a long innings with ITDC, she became its senior vice president. She speaks of her early experiences at the weekly:

'To be initiated into journalism by Khushwant was an experience that gave you a head start in the profession. I was lucky. In my training year at the TOI, I asked to be affiliated with *The Illustrated Weekly of India* and got it.

One day, Khushwant gave me a book of three short plays and asked me to write my comments. Was this a test? I wondered. The next week, I saw my comments in the magazine as a book review. I was delighted as my initials appeared under the review, although many of my long complicated words had been simplified and the sentences shortened.

"Remember, simple words and short sentences have the maximum impact," he told me. It was my first lesson. My editor treated each one as an equal. He made you slog till you got your facts right (there was no Google then, just the library) and your sentences right. He went through every caption and every word you wrote. Then he gave you credit through a much coveted by-line.

"Why do you have a pin up on the centre page of such an informative magazine?" I was cheeky enough to ask.He smiled and said he would take me out for lunch. As we walked down towards an Irani restaurant, he stopped at every vendor and asked him how many copies he had sold and what page he was exhibiting. The answer was always the same -- the pin-up page!

"Now you know. They buy the magazine for the attractive

centerspread and then read all the serious and informative articles as well", he declared. His marketing strategy was perfect. Our lunch outings became a regular feature and I was treated to a biryani and coke after each survey.

Like all really great men, Khushwant was humble and approachable. Many people took advantage of this. One day, he called me into his office and gave me a piece to edit. It had no heading. I took it out, edited it drastically, with critical remarks in the margins where I did not agree or cut out something, and took it back to his room. "Give it to my PA to type, with your changes and send down for printing", he said with a smile after a glance through it.

"But it has no heading, should I give one?" I asked.

"No need", he said with a straight face and added, "It is my edit."

I could have sunk through the floor. Only Khushwant could have let a trainee edit his Edit!

One fine day, I saw a list of titles for articles on my desk. Most titles had already been ticked by my senior colleagues. "This is a list of cover stories for 12 issues. You can pick one from the ones still available," Khushwant answered my query. I was awestruck. A young trainee doing a cover story for the highest selling magazine in India! It was a dream come true!

But only the seemingly dull titles were left. So I picked *The Sadhu Orders of India*, even though I was clueless about what it meant. Khushwant, the ace trainer came to the rescue. I was given lists of what to read, names of people to meet and appointments were fixed. He even came with me to the Ashram of the Brahmakumaris to show me how to interview.

Khushwant was a hard task master. I was drowned in clippings, library books and other research material. He checked every word I wrote and every photo. Six months later, when the story actually appeared, it was perfect and had my by-line! I was on top of the world.

Once Khushwant decided to mentor you, you were his responsibility for life. He was disappointed when I left journalism for a nine to five job in Delhi, as he had 'big plans' for me. He did not hesitate to reprimand my parents for pushing me into a traditional marriage, with its responsibilities!

Khushwant was always there for me. I would walk into his office or his home with my grumbles and my requests and he never said 'no'. He replied through his favourite yellow post cards to any written request and signed Chacha Khushwant.

In the last few years, I saw less of him, as I was enmeshed in my family and my work; he remained my pillar of strength and my Guru till the end.'

Chandni Luthra's experience of Khushwant's mentoring, informality and friendliness were repeated countless times as the highly successful editor of the weekly picked up young journalists and challenged them to their limit to bring out their talent and the hard work that they were capable of doing. It is seldom realised how hard Khushwant worked himself. Almost his entire life and to the last years, Khushwant had a routine of getting up at first light and sitting down to write at 5.00 am in the morning. This was a punishing routine and nobody ever saw that part of his life. As indeed, no one saw the tremendous amount of hard work and discipline that he put into his career, the long hours of reading and research, for which he was a stickler.

Khushwant took his journalism very seriously and worked hard at it in the various publications that he went to as the editor. One of his best media creations was the Amrita Bazaar Patrika group's *New Delhi* magazine. He assembled a group of fine young journalists to create the magazine from scratch. Everything that went into the magazine was his thinking and work.

Things got spectacularly brighter for Khushwant in 1980, when Mrs Gandhi came back to power, as it was payback time for his loyalty during and after the Emergency. He was frank enough about it and said, 'I expected to be rewarded for standing by them.' Along with Mrs Gandhi, Sanjay too was back in the driver's seat and he offered his largesse to the writer. An offer of the job of High Commissioner in London was turned down by Khushwant, as he wanted to stay back at Delhi. Then came the offer of editorship of the *Hindustan Times*, which Khushwant accepted. That indeed is how things work; editors of leading newspapers are mainly political appointments. However, what this also says for independent editors and freedom of the press is as clear as daylight. That was the system in India and Khushwant rode it to glory as editor of the country's top newspaper. He had no idea of working in, let alone running, a newspaper and soon realised there was not much he could do. But as was his habit, he worked hard from early morning to midnight every day, faced cynical opposition from the old and well entrenched staffers, and juggled the good honest journalism he wanted with politics in high places on one level, and the intrigues and union activities on another.

A liberal, easy-going editor

At the *Hindustan Times* too, he had loyal and promising journalists. One such journalist was a young reporter, Kumkum Chadha, whom he already knew. She was among those he was to encourage and mentor to the fullest blossoming of their talents. She was a committed investigative reporter who was to go on to become a redoubtable political commentator and columnist. Writing a brief foreword to her book, *Crucifixion*, a compilation of her incisive interviews with eminent newsmakers, Khushwant wrote that she was 'India's Oriana Fallaci', which was indeed a high praise for a young journalist to be compared to the famous Italian journalist known for her hard hitting interviews with international personalities.

Kumkum Chadha writes here about his HT days

'He was a liberal and an easy going editor, who made you feel comfortable and was open to new ideas. He was short on patience and had little time for mediocrity. Also, he was a stickler for time and schedules, so if you followed the punctuality principle, half the battle was won. For instance, if you were invited to his house for dinner, you had to be there at 7.00 pm sharp and leave by 8.45pm, not a minute late. If you tended to overstay, chances were you would be asked to leave with 'the party is over' remark. I don't think he was bothered about popularity or making headlines.

He was what he was and didn't give a damn about what people said or thought about him.That is why he was more misunderstood because he never bothered to correct any misconceptions or impressions and let people think what they wished. It didn't matter to him what the world thought of him. He wrote about serious issues, like his book on the Sikhs etc. He was a popular journalist and a good writer, who wrote simply and often touched a chord. He was often used by socialites to get him to write about them and he always found it difficult to say 'no' and that was his weakness. He had total lack of judgement on who should or should not be written about and, therefore, he often wrote about those who did not deserve to be written about. Soft hearted, as he was, he often praised their work, or almost negligible contribution, sky high and made the unknown famous. There were times when I, as also some of his family members, would point this out and he would laugh it off and say, "What could I do?" Yes, many took advantage of his goodness and soft heartedness, and clouded his journalistic judgements.

As an editor, Khushwant changed the rules, by way of timings and the way newspaper offices then functioned. He would be the first to arrive in office as early as 9.00 am, when even peons were not there, and would leave at 12 noon for lunch, when the reporters and other staff would start trickling in, and when he would be back by 2.00 pm, it would be lunch hour for all of us. And worse still, when it would be the hectic news time after 6.00 pm and the newsroom would be buzzing, he would call it a day. He was not the one who took kindly to phone calls; you could not really call him as and when you wanted. But he had systems in place and was a hands-on-editor who was accessible.'

One of the enigmatic and often drunk senior journalists at *Hindustan Times,* whom Khushwant mentions briefly in his autobiography, was Chand Joshi. He was a good writer but wrote a report only about once in three months. He was a card holding communist, usually busy with union activities and known to drink in the office on lazy afternoons. Khushwant steered clear of Chand, who was actually a very well read and sensitive writer, and an intellectual. 'He was a good friend', writes Vijay Narain Shankar, and though Khushwant gave him a wide berth, Chand admired the novels of the Sardar.

Once, while on his third drink at his haunt, the Press Club of India, Chand said to who? Onkar Singh? about Khushwant, 'He is a good and a deep writer, but wasting his time at the newspaper. When his political stock falls, as it will, for Sanjay Gandhi is true to no one.They will sack him. Mark my words.' Chand Joshi was right. Birla did not renew Khushwant's contract. It was the end of the phase of journalism for him, and for good. In the years ahead, he did what friends like Nirad Chaudhary had said he should have done exclusively all the time-writing.

The editorship of the *Hindustan Times* came and went with the politics of the day and Khushwant has had his moment of glory. As had happened at the weekly, so did it happen at the newspaper and, as before, it was politics that came in the way. He was to learn, as has many an editor before and after him, that the power and freedom of the editor is only as strong as one's employment contract. He had to leave. But something lasting, and of a great value, was that his Malice column, read now by millions of his countrymen in many languages, would continue.

The Khushwant column, appearing week after week in nearly fifty publications in a syndicated release, became bigger than almost anything else in the media at the time. Such a thing had never happened before. The column was eagerly awaited and read every weekend. More than the success that it brought him, the column also very largely shaped his style and choice of subjects for his popular writing in the years ahead. With the way the column shaped up in his choice of people and events, and the feedback he received week after week, Khushwant found a kind of formula that worked every time. It was controversy, sexuality, and kickass bluntness. The more he told people off for hypocrisy and sham, the more they loved it. He enjoyed his role, one that came naturally to him, of iconoclast and angry wise man.

What was happening with his Malice column was actually a comment on a strange quirk of the Indian psyche. Let us take Indian sexual attitudes as an example. People are prudish and hypocritical about sex and they know it. He told them that they had sex on their minds and they knew that too. There is obviously a lot of sexuality in India but kept desperately under wraps. They knew he was right in telling them off. But they couldn't help their mind-set and their conditioning. Although they criticised him yet they loved him for telling them off and for regaling them with sexual openness. It was strange but very simple. Most people (perhaps all is closer to the truth) enjoy sexuality. They called him things like 'dirty old man' and 'the sex obsessed Sardar' and it was all building him up into a popular legend. He loved it, as the success had come a little late late in his life. And he started working on it, not only in his columns, but also the flood of books that had titles like: *Sex, Scotch and Scholarship; On Women; The Company of Women;* and *Khushwant Singh on Women, Sex, Love and Lust.*

Khushwant was selling among people who would not normally be buying literary or heavy books. And so the publishers and Khushwant himself were cashing in on the run, which is not to say that he was not enjoying it. Right from his *Weekly* days, he had built up a reputation as a voyeur and, therefore, loved to flaunt his sexuality. His friends have been quick to say that he was not a dirty old man or a man with sex on his mind; he was no such thing. However, there is something of a defensive prudishness in that also. He was just a man, like most people, who had an usual kind of interest in sex and sexuality. He did not hide it and it gave him a reputation. Since he had that public image after the weekly, he probably decided to keep it as one of his specialities. And certainly, it got him a lot of readers.

One of his favourite stories about this love-hate of his fans bears repetition. The story was told by the writer himself in one of his columns: 'I also used to get a lot of hate mail. It did not upset me. However, one letter from Canada became a memento. It had the foulest Punjabi abuse accusing me of all manner of incestuous relationships. They were in Gurmukhi. Only the address was in English and very brief –Bastard Khushwant Singh, India. I was most impressed by the efficiency of the Indian postal service in locating the address of the one and only Bastard in the country.'

The joke books also came in this period of his populism and outsold all his other books. They were read by young and old alike and were sold in the biggest bookshops as well as on the pavements of city markets. Since all the jokes were, what are known as Sardar jokes, it was bound to happen that some Sikh groups would object to the lampooning of the community. The Sikh jokes had always been a form of popular humour in India before this but no one had seemed to mind. Now because Khushwant was a celebrity, and because very big money was involved, the protests started pouring in. So much so that the media bodies of the Akali Dal wrote to him to accept that he would refrain from making fun of the Sikhs. As was his style, Khushwant wrote them a postcard saying: 'Go to hell.'

He did not care that the joke books and the other sexy stuff were far away from literature or literary quality. Most critics think it strange that he did not care and, instead, produced books that or his protégées persuaded him to churn out. There were two reasons. Khushwant, as has often been said, lived comfortably in the highbrow and the lowbrow. And secondly, he had not only done his best and serious work, he was still doing it. Simultaneously, with books having 'sex and women and lust' in their titles, he was writing deeply thoughtful books on religion and God; he was writing novels like *The Sunset Club, Burial At Sea,* and the novel that he called his swan song, the panormic and ambitious, *Delhi-a Novel.*' He was also translating the works of greats of Urdu poetry, like Ghalib. So people could make their choice. A favourite question for the literati to deliberate upon was, 'who is the real Khushwant?' It was never answered.

Newspapers a rough ride for a writer

...But he set the blueprint for magazines

Superlatives have been heaped upon Khushwant for almost everything he did or wrote but the praise heaped upon him for his work in newspaper journalism was more of media hype and follow-the-leader adulation than a result of critical evaluation. It does not ever happen that everything a creative person does is great. For instance, Khushwant left his mark on journalism in his own way, but it is a bit farfetched to call him 'India's greatest journalist' or 'the journalist's journalist' at least as far as newspaper journalism was concerned. India has had some legendary editors like Chalapathi Rau, Pothan Joseph, Frank Moraes, Kuldeep Nayyar, Inder Malhotra and others, who have truly embellished the profession. A persistent cynicism and suspension of belief in people, a hard cynicism and an eye for political intrigues are essential for an editor who must deal, or at least try to deal, with facts and truths.

Khushwant was more a man of stories and human interest material. He was an editor who got deeply involved with people. To use the words of a *New York Times* writer, David Carr, who gave a fine description of an editor, Khushwant too was an editor who could 'create fine stories by typing on a keyboard of human beings, knowing which key to hit and how hard to press it is both art and craft.' As a journalist, he was not, and could not be, the hard boiled and cynical, ever distrustful media person that a normal newspaper correspondent or editor was at that time. He was more suited to magazines and when he became editor of *Hindustan Times*, eyebrows were raised and tongues wagged in the small community of the tough and the hard-headed political writers and editors who were strong political animals. In fact, it was his proximity to Mrs Gandhi that got him there and the other editors in the capital made no bones about this. He was never considered a career political editor. One reason of course was his 'insider status' with the Gandhi family. The other was that he did not have a long background of rising from the ranks, as all the other editors in major papers had done. They all had spent decades literally in junior jobs, as copy editors and beat reporters, and worked their way up.

Khushwant had not done any of that. His politics was too personal and he was much too involved with the political people he liked, mainly the Gandhi family. Newspaper journalists and editors seldom did that kind of personal alignment, at least not in the broad daylight. They were supposed to be, and usually were, neutral and objective. Khushwant on the other hand did openly write favourably biased stories on Mrs Gandhi and her son, Sanjay, and was their media adviser. He had made this quite clear with his unstinted support to the Emergency and defence of Sanjay Gandhi through thick and thin.

Adviser to Sanjay's *Surya* magazine

In fact, Khushwant became gratis adviser for Sanjay and Maneka's magazine *Surya* and made a number of quick trips to Delhi, at least twice or thrice a month, to work with the editors of that brain child of Sanjay and Maneka. He planned and rewrote articles for the initial issues of the magazine and, so even journalistically, he was totally identified with Sanjay Gandhi and the Congress party. Vijay Narain Shankar, co-author of this work and once the first editor of *Surya*, writes:

'Khushwant used to fly from Bombay and come to the *Surya* office at Tej Building, located on Bahadurshah Zafar Marg, which could be likened to Delhi's Fleet Street. The office was a temporary arrangement at the planning stage of the magazine.

Maneka also had her desk there. He used to walk in with Mrs Amteshwar Anand, Maneka's mother, who was a charming and pleasant person, as far as I was concerned, though Khushwant later found her to be haughty and over ambitious. Maneka was totally involved in the new magazine and Khushwant spent a lot of time giving ideas for the magazine. He wanted a great deal of research to verify every little fact and asked me to do an exclusive interview with Sanjay.

I met Sanjay a number of times and found him quiet and likeable. That is how he came across. Then once, Sanjay drove Khushwant and me to the Maruti factory near Gurgaon and I remember Khushwant saying: "Drive a bit slower. I don't want to go to my Maker yet." I did my interview initially along the drive and then at his factory, which was not big or very impressive. After a fortnight, my article on Sanjay was ready and Mrs Anand and her partner, a wonderful jovial lady called Ms Indira Dhodi, came with me to Bombay to meet Khushwant and some advertising people. Khushwant gave us all the time in the world. He thought my article was too emotional and lacked facts about Sanjay's goals and objectives. The impression I got was that my article did not praise or defend Sanjay enough. Khushwant was by then an out and out supporter of Sanjay. I did not really fit into a scenario of such adulation. A month later, I told Khushwant in Delhi that I was leaving

Surya. He did not like it. I had always admired him but, in this case, I felt disappointed, as he was not using his judgement, I thought.

At one time, it so happened that some pro-Congress party publications, among them *Surya* and *The National Herald*, received an anonymous packet of secret photographs. These were fully pornographic photographs, showing Jagjivan Ram's son in flagrant positions of sexual intercourse with a young girl. There were nearly a dozen pictures, totally obscene, and the pro-Congress party people were gloating over them, as it was a chance for them to get even with Jagjivan Ram, who was refusing to support Mrs Gandhi. The pictures had been sent to pro-Congress party papers, with the purpose of using them to blackmail him and get him back into the Mrs Gandhi camp. It was a dirty game and it was unfortunate that a great and clean man like Khushwant, though not involved in any way, was still among the players.

All of this went very much against Khushwant as a journalist. He was never a political writer in the sense of being an objective and analytical observer. While it was great that he followed his heart and gave unstinting loyalty, he backed Sanjay without exception. Even if he may have realised its implication at a later stage, he was too stubborn with an old world sense of loyalty to change his course.

We started calling him 'Khushamad' Singh

Editors like Kuldip Nayar, HK Dua and Inder Malhotra were among the top political journalists and writers of that time. It was widely believed that Nayar did not care much for Khushwant's journalism, a belief that the great editor has denied in his interview on these pages.

According to Nayar: 'Let us clear the air that Khushwant and I had misgivings; however, barring once, when he supported the Emergency imposed by Mrs Gandhi. This was after her seat was declared null and void, on 12 June 1975, by Justice Jagmohanlal Sinha of the Allahabad High Court, who found the Prime Minister guilty on the charge of misuse of government machinery for her election campaign. The court declared her election null and void, and unseated her from the Lok Sabha.We gave him a new name, Khushamad Singh. But in a matter of days, we stopped using that nickname.

Khushwant was fond of Mrs Gandhi and Sanjay, and even Maneka. When the latter was thrown out of the Prime Minister's residence on orders of Mrs Gandhi, Khushwant told the powerful Prime Minister that she may have thrown her out during the day, but she made the mistake of throwing her belongings at midnight. Maneka had tipped the press reporters who were present in a large number.

I first met Khushwant at Law College in Sialkot.This happened between 1945 and 1947, when he had returned home after getting the degree of Barrister from England.

He had been teaching law for eight years, but did not feel enthusiastic about it. He had a great command over English. He briefly joined Indian Foreign Service.

My dream of doing law was shattered by the partition of India in 1947. After those events and massacres, which he saw from both sides, Khushwant wrote *Train to Pakistan*.

The book was an instant success. But personally, I felt there was nothing in it.'

Nayar clearly was not the one to appreciate Khushwant's fiction and his dismissal of *Train to Pakistan* is very characteristic of a news-oriented journalist, who sees stories and intrigues in every little event that has to do with politics and politicians, but is usually not responsive to the kind of writing that Khushwant did. This is a bit surprising, because some very great novelists and fiction writers, amongst them Ernest Hemingway, started out as journalists or war correspondents. Their journey was exactly the reverse of Khushwant's. It is also commonly said that many wannabe writers actually start out with journalism. There are many examples of this. However, when a journalist becomes a political writer and gets involved with the machinations of people in power, he seems to move away from the more abstract and creative aspects of writing. Nayar had been the editor of *The Statesman* and other newspapers, and had made a name for himself with his book on political news and gossip, Between the Lines. It was an immediate bestseller way back in the 70s and revealed the life in the corridors of power, the horse trading and the comings and goings of opportunistic politicians. Nayar went on to become the Indian High Commissioner in London and retired after a most distinguished career.

To come back to Nayar's recollections of Khushwant: 'Khushwant went for a trip to Mumbai and here he had a chance meeting with Sahu Shanti Prasad. He had heard about the man and his capabilities. He made Khushwant the editor of the weekly, who continued to handle it for nine years. He was given a task to take the circulation higher than 60,000, which was under the British editors. He was given full freedom to write his column,With Malice Towards One and All. He was not bound by any rule and regulations.In no time, the weekly circulation jumped from 50,000 to four lakhs.

I always referred to him as Professor Sahib. On many occasions, Khushwant made sure that I was present during a dinner. He was afraid of his wife and his mother. Both were aggressive by nature.

When I was appointed as Indian High Commissioner in London, he called me up to inform that he would be visiting the UK and asked, 'Where would I stay?' I told him, 'Professor Sahib, you will stay with me.' He had best of Scotch during his stay. He was *dilare* (brave man) but also was a miser and would make sure he did not spend.'

Khushwant's time at the *Hindustan Times* was not such a great period, except for the fact that he developed his Malice column even more. The Malice column, and a few others that he created, were to become his mainstay in journalism after he left the newspaper. He was also nominated to the Rajya Sabha. That is how the editor was to be manipulated. He was sought to be manipulated while at the newspaper. This was in the matter of appointments and dismissals of staff, as well as coverage of stories, and political control, which he did not strictly comply. His non-compliance, as well as some of his views on government policies, made him unpopular in high places.

His own way of doing things

Be it the *Hindustan Times* or the Rajya Sabha, he managed to enjoy himself immensely for that was his way. In the house of the Elders, his seat was next to the actress, Nargis. He recounted that he had a hard job staying away from the farting MPs. When a communist MP, Bhupesh Gupta, called Khushwant a *chamcha* of Mrs Gandhi, he lost his temper and brought a complaint against the accuser, who was a doughty, stubborn customer. In the following debate, Khushwant sought to prove that his nomination was justified by his writing achievements and his prominence in society. After a good and convincing speech, he sat down. The communist MP rose to say that, no matter what Khushwant had to say, had to say, he stood by his remark that Khushwant was a *chamcha*. This infuriated Khushwant, who forgot he was in the august House of Elders, as he shouted: 'You are no gentleman, you bastard.' That was typical of Khushwant-impulsive and outspoken. The papers had the story the next day and Khushwant felt that he had let his side down.

Khushwant, at the biggest paper in the country, did not put on the pomp and status trappings of an editor. He had his own timings at the office; he thought the choice and presentation of his stories would get him success. He soon realised that an editor can do very little to really change a paper. His *Malice* column remained his biggest contribution. And then, as he recounted, he got 'Menon-gitis' for the second time in his life. A senior correspondent, NC Menon, crossed swords with Khushwant. Menon intrigued and carried stories to politicians and to KK Birla, as he eyed the editor's chair.

After Khushwant left the paper, the Malice column continued. He also developed other columns like 'This Above All' for *The Telegraph* and stayed on in journalism with bold strokes of his aggressive pen. Newspaper journalism was never his cup of tea and he was well away from it. The coming of television and digital media has perhaps made the newspaper less scoop oriented and competitive, but it was, in the 80s, a harsh battleground of political insiders, tips and newsbreaks from 'secret sources' and getting the news first.

The news journalist and the editor in the old days were a tough, hard drinking breed, and a lot of the drinking was done at press conferences and embassy parties. As one top newspaper editor, he was always seen at embassy and foreign parties, and was also gifted cartons of Scotch. It was said of him that he drank Scotch because he couldn't afford Indian whiskey. Khushwant was not from this world. He was truly a child at times who, when he got the news of his entry to the Rajya Sabha, ran from room to room of a magazine office, announcing it. He was 65 years old at that time.

At the office of the *New Delhi* magazine, where he became editor, he had a one-way glass pane installed in front of his room. He told the staff mischievously that he could see them but they could not see him. That was how he was. He saw the whole world and everything in it. But few could really see him. Another senior editor, who also edited the *Hindustan Times*, was HK Dua, who had also edited *The Indian Express* and *The Tribune* in Chandigarh.

Dua was a journalist of the old school, meticulous and with an eye for research and detail. Speaking of Khushwant, he said he met Khushwant once in a while and the writer had left a deep impression on him.

He was a perfectionist

Dua had this to say: 'He was a sort of perfectionist and he edited his own column Malice...three times before sending it to numerous newspapers and magazines. He believed in writing short sentences and took special care of commas and full stops, and where the para should begin and where it should end.

When I was editing *The Tribune,* he wrote a special column for my newspaper. I needed something new, as the *Malice* column was printed before us and, hence, we could not carry the same column. His writing became a hit and the Chandigarh gentry loved reading what he had to tell them.

Whenever he would go to Kasauli for few weeks/months, he would write on a postcard about his schedule and invited privileged people to a party. I being the editor-in-chief of *The Tribune* was one of the invitees. Even senior army officers were invited to join the party. He ensured all important persons were there to enjoy the lavish party.

The journalist community was upset when he wrote in favour of the Emergency in 1975. He liked Sanjay Gandhi and wrote in his favour. Sanjay took Khushwant to Gurgaon to the Maruti office. He was driven to all the places by Sanjay himself. Subsequently, he wrote in favour of the then Prime Minister Mrs Gandhi. He backed her action in strong language. Later on, he became the driving force behind Maneka Gandhi's new venture, *Surya India*. He was on it board of directors.

It is a general belief that he was appointed editor of the *Hindustan Times* and Sanjay was behind it. But I cannot say whether it is true or false. (Note: Khushwant has written in his autobiography that the post of editor of the *Hindustan Times* was arranged for Khushwant by Sanjay almost as soon as Mrs Gandhi came back to power in 1980.)

There is a family story in social circles that, when Khushwant returned to India, after getting the degree of Barrister, and was still flying high, someone asked his mother what did he do in London. She told them laughingly, 'I do not know what he has done there but one thing is sure, mauj karke ayya hai (he had a good time).'

Luck favoured him and he became India's most celebrated writer and journalist in no time. His novel *Train to Pakistan* became a hit and he became a well-known name abroad as well. He wrote about people and their plight,good fortunes as well as their hard struggle to have two square meals... His book *A History of Sikhs* (in two parts) is one of the best written books.'

The columns were syndicated and also translated into many Indian languages. He was a writer of great discipline and certainly the need to send out his columns on a regular basis became a routine, which he enjoyed. He often said that he never missed a deadline for his columns. What made these columns so spectacularly popular can be answered in one word—Khushwant. The political opinions or the outpourings of opinion on various social and lifestyle events were straightforward presentations of common sense.

He was, in turn, censorious, sarcastic, and at times angry with the humbugs, for things like corruption, political opportunism, and social ills, such as dowry, religious fundamentalism and hypocrisy.

He held up a mirror to his readers and they saw themselves in it, even as they read his columns week after week. They did not like what they saw, but they agreed with the angry Sardar, that was all. In India, life goes on as before and people are quite happy in just knowing that they know what is wrong with them. The columns became a kind of conscience drug that Khushwant delivered to his vast readership every week; he became a high priest of good sense. It was the column again and the often outrageous opinions; outrageous because they were brave in the face of smug Indian attitudes, which made him a household name. People took him very seriously even though he laughed at them. But that was just his way. He did not even take himself very seriously though he was a tremendously serious man.

Almost every journalist in India, and foreign correspondent found it necessary to meet and interview Khushwant. He was an eminent and an intellectual landmark of Delhi and it was impossible to ignore him. Apart from the acclaim and recognition that his books gave him, it was also his columns and his stints in journalism that gave him this position.

One of the best known of the foreign correspondents in

Delhi, Mark Tully[2] of the BBC, has pleasant recollections of his meetings with Khushwant.

He had a wonderful sense of humour

Superfluous Mark said, 'I liked Khushwant very much. I admired him but I didn't know him all that well. As the BBC correspondent in Delhi, I interviewed him for programmes. As a freelance journalist after I left the BBC, I was the last person to interview him. I always found him very welcoming. We would have a glass of whiskey together after the interview if it was in the evening.'

When asked which books of Khushwant did he like best, Mark said, 'I particularly liked his book *Nature Watch*, about the flora and fauna of Delhi. He was very knowledgeable about trees and plants, and wrote about them so well. Like so many others, I thoroughly enjoyed his classic novel, *Train to Pakistan*, and learnt so much about the Partition from it. When Satish Jacob and I wrote our book on *Operation Blue Star*, Khushwant's *A History of Sikhs* was our main source for the historical chapter.'

When asked about the novel, *Delhi*, Mark says, 'To be honest, I didn't care for it.'

When asked about his thoughts about Khushwant as a

---

[2]Sir William Mark Tully, the BBC correspondent in India for over twenty years, was born in Calcutta in the days of the Raj. He has been living in India since his retirement and has written a number of books on India.

journalist, Mark replied, 'He was a great editor. He expanded the circulation of *The Illustrated Weekly* dramatically and made it the magazine that you had to read. He trusted his reporters and gave them great freedom. They rewarded him with loyalty and affection.'

Khushwant was given the title of dirty old man, for writing about his adventures with the fairsex during his stay in London. His column With Malice towards One and All led prudish Delhites to talk disparagingly about him. Mark was asked about his thoughts on this and he replied, 'Khushwant enjoyed the company of women, as he frequently admitted, and women greatly enjoyed his company, but I don't think that, in reality, he was a dirty old man. I liked his columns. They were delightfully irreverent and often very funny.'

Mark was asked about his views on the criticism that Khushwant attracted due to his favourable views on the Emergency and he replied, 'In a funny way, I rather admired him for this. I did talk to him about it and got the impression that he really believed that the Emergency was necessary and although he knew that he was swimming against the tide and that, for the most part, his fellow journalists disapproved of his views, he had the courage to publish them.'

On Khushwant's personal life, Mark said, 'I don't know a lot beyond what everyone knows. He was a much disciplined man, famously getting up very early to play tennis and going to bed early. He would only attend dinner parties if food was served in time for him to go to bed early. I do remember attending one dinner party in his flat where we were all told to go home long before the normal time Delhi dinner parties end. He enjoyed Scotch whiskey but was a disciplined drinker. He loved Urdu poetry and, almost at the end of his life, I went to a *mushayra* in his flat where Saeed Naqvi recited poetry. Although he was by then quite weak, he thoroughly enjoyed it. When I look back, I would say he was a unique character, who had a wonderful sense of humour.'

A truly unique and timely contribution was made by him when he changed the old *The Weekly*. He brought in human interest stories, contemporary happenings and personalities and, of course, a new attitude to sexuality and liberal lifestyles. In a sense, he liberated Indian magazines from the old concept of stultified, conservative culture, which only meant classical music and dance, and highbrow arts. That was his big contribution. He came to the scene when journalism was changing with the changing world. By the time he left the weekly, television had come to India and magazines like *India Today* were rolling out. By then, the weekly and *Filmfare* had been the only English magazines along with a very few language publications. By the year 1980, nearly a dozen magazines in English had appeared in India and many more were on the way. They came with colour, new-fangled design ideas, much more lively style of headlining and writing, and it can be said that globalisation started with magazines just before it came to the country. All these magazines had good, young journalists and creative people working for them. Yet it can truthfully be said that the blueprint for all these new Indian magazines had been put together by Khushwant.

A most unbelievable kind of loner

Life and its living was the important thing

Writers can be inveterate egotists, for there is a kind of intellectual narcissism that drives them deeper and deeper into their own worldview. Perhaps all artists must have this sense of something that they must give in return to the world and for which they must perhaps move away from the ordinary and the mundane. There is a single-mindedness of purpose in spite of being involved in the business of living. Khushwant, like many great creative people, had a great passion for life and for living it to the full, but like them, he also had the ability to withdraw at will and be with himself. People close to him have all said that he remained a loner, which would be unbelievable to people who only saw the public image that he had.

Even as the writer travelled and lived at places all over the world in his early life, his family travelled with him and he enjoyed the company of two children, Mala and Rahul, and his lovely wife, Kawal, who made a home for him wherever he went. Soon after he resigned from his job at the Indian High Commission in London, he was at low ebb, since he had decided to take up writing but did not have a clue as to how it would go. He wrote, 'I had saved up money which could last me about six months. I had also kept away a stock of my favourite Scotch whiskey that would see me through.' He had to send away his family from London as he embarked on his venture of writing full-time. 'I missed the children running about in the house and was on my own,' he has said. His children, who grew up to be writers in their own right, stayed close to him all his life.

Kawal, his wife, was efficient and highly protective, keeping the world away from him, as he concentrated on writing. In his later years, right from 5 o'clock in the morning to the final hours of the day, Khushwant was in his house, sprawled in his living room, which was a mess of piled up books and pieces of paper; he shut himself off mentally from the world. It was she who saw to his every comfort, disciplined him to a large extent and he readily submitted. Where there had been love in their youth, there was also a deep affection between them, which accepted each other's shortcomings and enjoyed the things that were good. When she passed away, eight years before him, Khushwant was devastated. He spent that night alone, sitting up in a dark room and thinking, though he really did not know what to think anymore. As an agnostic, who did not believe in God or the afterlife, he had no consolation of believing that she would exist in any way after her passing. 'I did not know, and nobody knows, where people come from and where they go,' he was to say later. He also decided, in the extreme darkness of his grief, that he would not write any more. Writing was all that his life had been in essence. And yet, in the sorrow of her passing, that was the one most precious thing that he thought he should snatch away from himself. As it happened, however, this was not to be and, after some time, he picked up his pen and paper again.

A fine man to know

Speaking of her father, Mala Singh Dayal says: 'I enjoyed the same privileges as my brother, Rahul, and our father never discriminated. I was allowed to visit the same colleges where Rahul had studied. Yet my father was strict and loved to live a disciplined life.'

Mala is tall like her father and has spent her life as a writer as well as looking after the publishing house set up by her husband, Ravi Dayal. 'My father had no idea that I had an affair with Ravi Dayal. He was busy editing *The Weekly* when, at the age of 27 years, one fine morning I decided to break the news that I had found a man who I was marrying in a week's time. Obviously, the news shook him a bit, but he recovered in no time and asked me who was going to be my husband. Once he knew, he readily gave his consent.

My father had developed a personality, which gave the impression that the great Khushwant Singh was a lady killer. I personally feel he was happy to allow this impression to grow merely to capture attention of his readers,' Mala put it politely. She named a couple of women who tried to get attention by remaining glued to him whenever one of his books was released, in order to get themselves in pictures and trying to impress their friends that they were so close to Khushwant.

Mala added: 'I was hospitalized for treatment of cancer for some time. I later learnt that my loving father had given up eating. His health had dropped and the moment I was out of hospital, I went to see him and his face lit up. Naina, my daughter, forced him to eat and fought with him and left instructions what to do and what not to do. Once, when Naina was late, my father kept pacing in his room up and down till she showed up. He strongly felt that she should not be home after it gets dark.

Everything was not well with him in his writings. The day he wrote a piece on LK Advani, a fundamentalist in his own right, we were all aghast. We greeted him with slogans of Jai Sri Ram. He took the message. Some of his readers felt that Khushwant used to make provocative statements in his write ups in the weekly only to create controversies so that more people read what he had written about some of the political personalities. Some believe he would often withdraw his controversial statements. But we know, for a fact, that some of the cases registered against him are still pending in the court of law.'

Both Mala and Rahul were very close to their father all their lives and such was the impression the great author made upon his children that both became writers and have been active in the media. She has written a large number of books for children, that are rich with fantasy and imagination. She has also put together books of Khushwant's writings in a steady stream that celebrates the work of her father. The book, *Me the Jokerman*, was a collection of over fifty essays, most of them unpublished in book form, on religion, nature, sex, autobiography, and humour. Another book that was produced to celebrate his writing was '99 *Unforgettable Fiction, Non-fiction, Poetry and Humour.*' Staying close to her father's house in Sujan Singh Park in central Delhi, Mala was a rock of support to Khushwant in his last days and saw to all his needs, with care and affection. In one of his last books, Khushwant wrote of living alone in his house after his wife's passing away and expressesd the thought that he hasd become a burden on his granddaughter, Naina, who was the apple of her grandfather's eye. When Naina was a little girl, Khushwant enjoyed playing with her nearly *30 Cats*. In his last years, she made it a point to visit Khushwant almost every day.

Mala collected and edited a book of tribute to her father on his hundredth birth anniversary, which he missed celebrating by just one year. The book, *Portrait of a Serial killer*, is a collection of his unpublished writings, his wanderings among celebrities and film stars, and his constant sardonic astonishment at the way ordinary people perceive the famous. There are some gems from the pen of Khushwant in this book that remind us of his keen observation of people.

After a meeting with the actor, Dev Anand, Khushwant had this to say: 'The almost full bottle of Black Dog was evidence that the Scotch had not been drunk...Dev had nursed his own Scotch and soda. When it was time to go, I hauled myself up from the sofa, while Dev, only a few years younger than I, leapt up like a coiled spring. His fight against age is a little pathetic...He strode ahead of me, his pace of walking as fast as his speech. I trailed behind... and heard the hallowed name, Dev, being intoned.'

Khushwant's meeting with the Nightingale of India, Lata Mangeshkar, also had some humour for him. He found her gentle and very shy, and yet asked her to let him have her autobiography for serialisation in the weekly. As he got up to leave, Khushwant saw the *Filmfare* award statuettes—black ebony statues, about a foot high, of a nude female figure. He was amused to notice that nude statuettes in her home had been draped with mini silk saris to cover their nakedness.

Included in this book is the story Khushwant wrote about Mrs Gandhi's 'non-existent' Sable Mink coat, which had been much talked about in the media. The coat was a figment of imagination, as a mink coat worth a million dollars never existed then.

In his later years, he wrote about his having to live alone, as his wife had passed away in her mid-80s. He wrote: 'Though we were prepared for her death, but when it came, we were shattered...I could not bring myself to light her funeral pyre. In the absence of my son, my daughter lit it on our behalf.' His wife had asked that no ceremony be performed after her death and so there were no prayers said. 'I had to cope with my loss with whatever inner resources I could muster. The first night (on the day of her death) was the longest in my living memory. I sat in my armchair, switched off all the lights and talked silently to myself. I had to teach myself how to live alone in an empty home. I broke down many times. By morning I was exhausted.'

He spoke of their sixty-two year old marriage as one that had its ups and downs and yet they evolved a routine of life that suited them both. 'My wife was very houseproud. She taught our cook how to prepare gourmet quality dishes…I had to be left alone for many hours every day to write. We met at meal times and took our evening walks together in Lodhi Park.' Though much has been written about his so-called 'unhappy marriage', the fact is that it was mainly the media that built up this salacious story. Khushwant had been frank about the joys and the problems of his marriage, and that is something that probably exists in every marriage that lasts for as many years as his life with his Sardarni had lasted. 'Within a fortnight of her death, though,' he writes, 'I had made terms with my having to live alone. I am fortunate in having a daughter living next door, who make sure my health remains stable…I am now over ninety and have become dependent on my children and friends.'

Khushwant also wrote about his grand-daughter, Naina. He said: 'I am unduly attached to my only grandchild. I am doing my best to distance myself from her. I believe in the Buddha exhortation that one must shed all worldly attachments.'

Naina, went on to become a professor of history and is now the head of the department at St Stephen's College, the college where Khushwant was educated. She remembers the walks she had with her grandfather when she was a little girl. She talks of the walks in Lodhi Garden that would turn into impromptu lessons on architecture of the old monuments:

'In my early childhood, Nana did some grandfatherly things. He would get me chocolates, ice cream and Campa Cola. He also did some non-grandfatherly things. During our walks in Lodhi Garden, he identified plants and birds. He told me about the Lodhis and the architecture of Bada Gumbad Masjid…By the age of three, I knew such things as the Latin name of madhumalati and many more details about the First Battle of Panipat.'

His love for nature and history was easily transmitted to the younger ones in the family. His nephew also talks about the history lessons given by Khushwant when he was a young boy. Naina was also very strict with him, especially about what he ate and drank when he was much older. In his last years, recalls Mala with a laugh, 'he would say, "*paani nahin peena, Pepsi lao*," (I don't want to drink water, get me some Pepsi).'

Asked by a journalist whether the house in Sujan Singh Park, where he lived and worked all his life, would become a museum, Mala replied: 'Never, museums are dead places. In fact, we are painting the house. My daughter, Naina, has started to change the pictures in the drawing room…She wants to bring it back to some extent to what it looked like when my mother was around.' Indeed, it is a thoughtful decision by those who loved him the most, for Khushwant would never belong easily in any kind of museum. All those who knew him, and even those who read him, can never pass by Sujan Singh Park without thinking of him and without feeling that he is going to be present among the living, in their memory.

Perhaps, his daughter, Mala, says it all when she writes in the preface to *Portrait of a Serial Killer:* 'As I was reading the essays, I was struck by the many facets of my father that I was aware of but had not given much thought to...He was not just an excellent writer and a journalist, but also a man of integrity, with an unshakeable belief in doing what was right. An unusual human being; he was not a nice man to know, but a fine man to know.'

A very simple man

Khushwant was exceedingly simple in his ways. Writer and film critic, Amita Malik, had once called him the worst dressed man in India. Khushwant laughed at that and such was his careless way of dressing that he made sure that what she said was true. His usual dress was a cotton trouser and a faded T-shirt, when he was working. The house he lived in was comfortable but without any of the modern glitz. It was kept spotless clean but, in later years, it fell into his careless ways and was chock-a-block with books and papers. In fact, at times, when he went for his book launches, which he loved, or did the occasional appearance on television, he had to be persuaded to shed his old clothes and wear new ones. A friend recalls that, once when he won a court injunction against the publication of his autobiography in a case launched by Maneka Gandhi, Khushwant celebrated by ordering a brick of ice cream.

He had no wish for or longing for the high life, the consumerist opulence of India after globalisation, which he saw all around him and disliked. He often lamented the changes that had taken place in Delhi, with its profusion of cars and traffic jams. He rarely, if ever, went out to eat in restaurants or five star hotels. His tastes were simple and, as is the case, with the people of an older generation of Indians, there was no hankering for the splurge of excitement, the frenzy to buy things just because they appeared on the market. In fact, the Delhi that he loved all his life, almost a romantic old love for a beautiful woman, that Delhi had totally changed by the 1980s. There was a time when friends recalled that he used to drive around in his small Maruti car and enjoy himself on the uncrowded roads of the city. He could not do that once the cars flooded the roads. However, he still wanted to live in Delhi and only went to his villa in Kasauli for the summer. In fact, when he was offered a choice, by Sanjay Gandhi in 1980, between a job as Indian High Commissioner in London or editorship of the *Hindustan Times*, he declined the job in London because he did not want to leave his beloved city.

A hero to his chef

It is said that no man is a hero to his valet. In Khushwant's case, that may not have been exactly the case, as he wrote to his chef and man Friday of many decades, Chandan Singh,

82, of Tehri Garhwal. Khushwant was well loved and well-remembered by the old man who served them for so many years. We thought it would be interesting to talk to the chef about Khushwant's likes and dislikes as it is also true that few people know a man as well as his personal attendant.

Chandan Singh said proudly that he was not restricted to the servant quarters and was allowed to have lunch and dinners at the family table, after Khushwant and others had finished. As a 17-year old lad, when he landed in Delhi in search of a job, Chandan had no idea about what was cooking in his life. Khushwant's mother (Sir Sobha Singh's wife) asked him to lend a helping hand in cooking to an old chef. So he actually started working for Khushwant's father. 'Khushwant Sahib used to join his mother and father during lunch and dinner. The system continued for three years and, one fine morning, he came and asked me to come with him. From that day onwards, I became his personal *cook*,' soft spoken Chandan said, as he wiped tears.

'Sahib ji would go to bed by 10 pm and rise at 4 am in the morning and then head straight for drawing room, where he was served with a cup of tea. Having finished tea, he would pick up his pen and writing pad and start working on his new column. The newspapers arrived at 5.30 am in the morning. He would stop writing and scan them for news, particularly, any political development. Having read the papers, he would get up from his legendary chair and get ready to practice tennis at Delhi Gymkhana. Leander Paes and Kiran Bedi were some of his sparring friends. He played for half an hour before driving back to his Sujan Singh Park residence. In breakfast, he loved to have bread with butter, with tea or coffee, according to his mood.'

Whenever Khushwant moved to Kasuali, he made sure Chandan was sent off first and reached the destination in advance, then cook and keep the lunch or dinner ready, depending on what time Khushwant had to arrive. Khushwant loved to eat chicken and was also fond of fish. In winters, he loved to have *macce ki roti* and *sarson ka saag*, with lots of white butter, if available. He loved to eat *gajjar ka halwa* and sometimes offer it to his guests, which was very rare.

'Clear directives about what to cook for lunch and dinner came from Madam (Kawal). If guests were coming for dinner, she would make several rounds in kitchen to make sure that things were under control. I would like to mention that my two sons got their jobs because Sahibji spoke to some people who were in a position to help. I am indebted to him for his kind gesture. I wish my pay was at par with the serving employee in the house.'

Prominent persons who accepted his dinner invitations included former Prime Minister Indira Gandhi; former President of India, Zail Singh; Sanjay and Maneka Gandhi; former Prime Minister Rajiv Gandhi, and his son Rahul;

former Chief Minister of Punjab, Surjeet Singh Barnala, and hundreds of other dignitaries.

'There is one thing that stands out-Khushwant Sahib did not wish bad for anyone. He was a large hearted person and spoke well of everyone. He was not a person who would say something when you were with him and say another thing when you were gone.

When he was pleased with my cooking, he would pat my back,' Chandan concluded with a broad smile.

Love for Delhi

Khushwant wrote a number of books on Delhi.

His book, *City Improbable: Writings on Delhi,* was a collection of writings about his wanderings through the old and the new city.

His other book, *Delhi-a Portrait*, which Khushwant did with a well-known photographer, Raghu Rai, was a highly acclaimed work, as it brought together two fine talents in a representation of a city that has existed for many centuries, is ancient as well as modern. The book covered the monuments and the old lanes of the walled city, as well as its people, including pictures of some famous artists, like Ustad Amjad Ali Khan playing the Sarod at the Red Fort; scenes from the riverside of the city; the human faces and expressions through which the photographer and the writer tried to bring out the very soul of a modern city, seamlessly having its roots in a living past.

Another book on Delhi was *Celebrating Delhi*, in which there were writings by Khushwant, author William Dalrymple and others. In this book, the chequered history of the city has been brought out, a city repeatedly populated and abandoned, invaded and brutalised, and yet survived to synthesise and create its own culture.

Khushwant also gave some memorable lectures on Delhi, in which he spoke of the old city, and the making of the new one by his illustrious father, Sir Sobha Singh, who built much of what is now known as New Delhi. His father was present at the Delhi Durbar in1911, at which King George V declared that the capital of British India would be shifted from Calcutta to Delhi. 'Rarely was a man so identified with the birth of a city as Sir Sobha Singh was with New Delhi, translating into sand stone and marble most of the imperial blueprints of the architects. Few builders in the world have left behind, as tributes to their genius, such an imposing list of edifices, encompassing most of the colonial face of Delhi, as he has done,' said Khushwant. His talks and lectures at various events, in and outside the country, were also highlights of a writer who extended himself and had opinions to offer on almost everything. He taught at, or gave lectures, at mass communication organisations. He was also a visiting lecturer at universities of Oxford, Princeton, Hawaii and Calgary among others. One of his favourite subjects was Sikhism, as he was considered an authority, following the publication of his historical book, *A History of Sikhs.*

Wherever he went, Khushwant could not be but himself. He had earned for himself the reputation of being a 'Sassy Sardar' and was no stranger to controversy. As in his writings, so was it with his appearances, that social events and cultural organisations where he spoke, he created some controversy. He created a furore with his remarks on Shivaji, when he was in Mumbai. Facing threats to his life, he had to buckle down and apologise. At another time, at a workshop on journalism in Shillong, Khushwant created mayhem. Commenting on the works of Rabindranath Tagore, he said that the great Bard of Bengal, a Noble Prize winner, was 'a writer of no great merit.' Only Khushwant could have said this. The next day, the local newspapers carried the story headlining it: Khushwant Singh lampoons Tagore. Newspapers everywhere picked up the story, and politicians and leaders in Calcutta screamed in a masala protest. Khushwant later did say that he had read the Indian translations of several works of Tagore and did not find them to be much. However, he also said that, when he did read a better translation, he thought that Tagore was indeed profound. That was his only apology. He also said: 'A writer is meant to be read, not worshipped.'

I keep no secrets

Though he tried to conserve his time and spent most of it in reading or writing, which was the main theme of his life, he was by nature a gregarious and social person. This was one of the interesting paradoxes of his quicksilver intellect. He was social and yet he was an intensely private person in his literary and intellectual life. As in everything else, where he was like a rope stretched between extremes and diversities of existence, his was an effortless balancing act.

David Davidar, a close friend, and a prominent publisher and a fine novelist himself, says it best when he talks of the three lives of Khushwant. Building on the Gabriel Garcia Marquez thought that all men have a public, a private and a secret life, David says: 'These three lives of Khushwant infused every aspect of his writing. They gave it its honesty, originality, humour, immediacy, accessibility, pugnacity and brilliance.' His public life comprised the whirl of activity in the corridors of power; friendship with celebrities in film, business, publishing and journalism; and appearances at social and cultural events. His private life was his home and his work. And like all men, he had a secret life, though he did not keep it much of a secret, of unabashed sexuality, friendships with his 'unforgettable women' and something that few ever came to know-his habit of deep thought and of being a witness to people and their deepest selves.

Much has been made of his extremely frank and explicit writing about matters related to sex, alcohol, and morality. This was something that continues to shock mainly Indian readers who are not really used to such frankness. However, it was not in his nature, nor his style, to be smug and pompous. He once wrote: 'If you write fearlessly and candidly, you have to be prepared to pay the price. And there is no point writing if you are not honest...I have always written what I felt and believed to be true...There is no secret I kept to myself...At times this has upset people but I have never been bothered.'

He wrote explicitly even about his marriage, about the ups and downs and certain events that most men would not like to talk about publicly. As David Davidar suggests, this frankness of Khushwant, about his personal life, reminds one of the total honesty that was shown by Gandhi in his own autobiography, where he talked of an episode of passion with his wife. Such extreme honesty is not always seen in most writers when it comes to their personal lives. When Khushwant was writing his autobiography, 'Truth, Love and A Little Malice', the story goes that he spoke to his daughter, Mala, since she had been the one who had persuaded him to write the book in the first place. She advised him that he should write it just the way he wanted to. An early chapter of the book shows his wife in a slightly negative light. He said that he intended to write the book as honestly as he could.

Such honesty had little place in the Indian environment of smug hypocrisy. Sometimes, the reactions of the moral brigade to Khushwant were quite hilarious. An MLA from Uttar Pradesh once wrote angrily that Khushwant was at an age when he should be telling people to live with high moral values, abstain from the pleasures of life, and think of the hereafter. He was, however, doing the opposite and 'talking about unholy things.'

Such reactions were common and concerned Khushwant's insistence on flaunting his great enjoyment and love for the company of women.

The company of women

In his novel, *The Company of Women,* Khushwant seems to outdo himself in sexual explicit passages. He had often said that we have sex on our minds and it is certainly true that, at least for his popular books, which came in his later years, he dabbled in a lot of sexual fantasy. It would not be far wrong to say that, in his simple and honest manner, he was a lovable phony in the matter. He was disarmingly clever about his book titles, and the words 'sex 'and 'lust' appear often in them. Usually, there is hardly any eye-popping 'sex' or 'lust' there. The words were part of his armoury for popularity. A comment made by a journalist, Dhiren Bhagat, on this matter was affectionately wicked, when he said that he doubted whether Khushwant, especially in his later years, had slept with anything more interesting than a hot water bottle.

His real friends knew this and accepted it as the whimsy of a writer. Khushwant knew the world and mixed easily with people. But he had few friends. Among them was writer Nirad C Chaudhri who, in his intensity and intellectual and profound statements, was very different from Khushwant's lightness of personality. Khushwant had a great admiration for Nirad. A long time ago, Khushwant asked Nirad to write for a government publication on a subject which he knew well. Nirad had earlier been put under a ban by the government for something he had written. However, the ban had since been lifted. Nirad's answer was typical of the proud and diminutive Bengali writer. He said to Khushwant: 'The government has lifted the ban on Nirad but Nirad has not lifted the ban on the government.' Recalling this, Khushwant said, admiringly, that Nirad was living almost in poverty at that time and could have used the money, but his self-respect was more important.

Soli Sorabjee, former Attorney General of India; Mrs Charanjeet Singh, hotelier and owner of Le Meridien in Delhi; novelist Ruth Pravar Jhabavalla and her architect husband were other long-time friends who met him off and on. Mostly, they met him in the mid-mornings, a time for the real Khushwant.

Even when he was well into his 90s, Khushwant had a regular soiree at his residence every evening, at which at least half a dozen beautiful young ladies were always present. They included writers, diplomats, poets and talented creative women, who found him great company. Khushwant, needless to say, had his one fondness of intellectual and humorous sparring with these ladies, as he sipped his peg or two of single malt. Many among these ladies became acknowledged and well-known writers themselves, perhaps with a little help from Khushwant, who put in a good word here and there, or did a bit of mentoring. He cared not a bit for the usual raised eyebrows and censorious gossip and, in fact, we feel sure that he revelled in it.

It was felt sometimes that the old man was, in fact, being used by some of these socialites, and they were unjustifiably criticised. The fact is that, apart from his own family that looked after him for all his needs, Khushwant found a certain companionship, perhaps even a boost to his ego, certainly some evenings of banter and happiness, in the company of these women friends. They, in fact, did benefit from their association with him. But to say that they became writers because of him is far from the truth. If they did not have the talent, and the intellect, they would not have been publishing books long after his demise. One of the ladies, also a regular at his evening soirees, Kamna Prasad, had an abiding interest in the Urdu literature. When she met Khushwant, she found a kindred soul in the writer, for he had been a lover of Urdu poetry all his life.

He encouraged her in her mission of working for Urdu and collaborated with her in producing a rich volume of Urdu poetry, *Celebrating the Best of Urdu Poetry.* It was published by Penguin and, quite certainly, a word from Khushwant must have helped. A word from him to publishers and others, in the world of books, would certainly have helped a lot of men and women writers.

We learned a lot at his feet

Writing in the *Hindustan Times* after his death, Kamna Prasad opens with an emotional line in Urdu: 'aisa kahan se layen ki tujhsa kahen jise...' (from where can we get someone for whom we can say that he is like you). This talented lady is one of many writers, from across both genders, who were encouraged and helped by Khushwant. She writes: 'There is and will be nobody like him. He taught us how to celebrate life, how to live every moment of life...I came from Bihar and didn't know anybody in Delhi at that time. I met him and, through him, I met everybody else…He touched my life in a big way and I owe him a great deal for what I am today... *'unke kadmon mein baith kar bahut kuch seekha'*…(sitting at his feet, I have learnt so much). Khushwant participated actively as a patron of the Jashn-e-BaharTrust run by her, which works to popularise the Urdu language.

Neelima Dalmia Adhar is also an author, who remembers how helpful Khushwant was when she wrote a book on her father, RK Dalmia, who had once been the owner of *The Times of India*. Khushwant knew Dalmia well and, as she recounts, the writer regaled her with stories of her father getting his hour-long oil massage by two skilled masseurs while he met his officers and executives, and conducted his business. He also told her about her stepbrother, who had a one-sided love affair with Khushwant's daughter and wooed her with truckloads of roses and biscuits, manufactured by a biscuit company owned by her father. She met Khushwant with a manuscript of her book, *Father Dearest*, which had been commissioned by a publisher. Khushwant's first reaction was to give her an amused look and he said: 'I hope you haven't deified him. Syrupy stories about loving fathers of spoiled children make me ill...But let me read it.' She gave him the manuscript and being a young writer, and anxious to know his reaction, she kept on asking him about it. 'But did you like it?' she once asked. 'Stop fishing, young lady. I'm totally gripped,' he said. That, she says was the most euphoric moment of her life. He later made a mention of her book in his Malice column.

She says in her article, Let's Not Mourn Khushwant Singh' that, on the many evenings she spent at his house, Khushwant joked about her being a useless teetotaller. However, she remembers absorbing a wealth of knowledge merely by being there. She writes: 'His blatant mockery of death and his devil-may-care handling of all matters pertaining to life and God warrant only celebration. His passing on is no cessation of his omniscience...To mourn his death at the glorious age of ninety-nine years, a life that he lived giant size, is indeed being irreverent to him... 'bagh e bahisht se mujhe hokum-e-safar diya tha kyon; kare jahan daraz hai, ab mera intezar kae (Why did you send me out from the garden of paradise? I have work to finish, now you will have to wait for me)."

Someone who has fond memories of Khushwant's encouragement and mentoring is one of our greatest editors, and currently a minister in the Union Cabinet, MJ Akbar. He was a young man in 1971, when he went to *The Weekly*, with dreams of journalism. He writes:

'The media here keeps those on the first rung of the ladder, scratching around for years. Khushwant lifted them to the top with a carefree shrug, but with a very, very careful eye on the copy they submitted.

I have no idea what life had in store for me if Khushwant, and his wonderful deputy editor, Fatima Zakaria, had not offered me the chance that changed my fortunes. But this I do know, what they did was enough to command a lifetime's gratitude... He pretended not to believe in God, but I do fancy that God certainly believed in him.'

War on 'fundoos' and the communal discourse

He felt fundamentalism would be the end of India

'If there is one regret,' said Khushwant in his later years, 'it is that I did not write more in my columns against the fundamentalists who are destroying India.' He wrote books about this belligerent breed of Theo-fascists and bigots, the angriest of them being his book, *The End of India*. This book was published into many language editions and its passionate condemnation of all kinds of fundamentalists —he deprecatingly dubbed them 'fundoos'—brought him hate and criticism. He did not care, of course, and it set him apart from a lot of journalists and writers who teetered on the razor's edge of political correctness and not sticking their necks out too far. Khushwant said it as it appeared to him; India after the 80s had become the violent and malevolent battleground of communal organisations and political parties.

'The nineties were dark times for India. Fascism well and truly crossed our threshold and dug its heels in our courtyard. We let the fanatics get away with every step they took without raising a howl of protest. They burnt books they did not like; they beat up journalists who wrote against them; they openly butchered people for believing in a different God.' (Khushwant Singh, *Absolute Khushwant*, 124).

He wrote in a cold fury about the Advani juggernaut of *Rath Yatras* that ended in historical communal divide caused by the Babri masjid demolition. He rued the Hindutva vigilantes who attacked liberal dissenters, killed rationalist intellectuals and forced one of India's greatest artists, MF Hussain, to live in exile. Khushwant had seen the worst of communal violence during Partition. He had thought then that, in the bloodshed, rapine and breakdown of all humanity, it was the end of India, as the country was torn apart. He had to see it again and again, and was convinced that it would destroy India.

Memories of Partition

In 1947, he was in Lahore when the communal violence erupted. He saw the killings and the deadly communal battles on the streets from his rooftop. These events occurred midway in the month of June. He recalled that there were wild shouts and exploding sounds of gunfire as mobs came out on the street. From one end came Muslims, who were armed with knives and lathi sand shouted *Allah-O-Akbar*, and from the other end came the Hindus shouting *Har Har Mahadev* and the Sikhs with their warlike *Boley-So-Nihal*, in blood curdling voices. The Hindus and Sikhs had started leaving the Muslim dominated towns to come to Lahore but, on finding it unsafe, they marched on to cross the border and found refuge in towns of eastern Punjab. In his own words: 'I ran up to the roof of my apartment…A huge cloud of dense black smokc billowing out…The Hindu-Sikh locality nearby was going up in flames….'

'We remained mute spectators to the Muslim league supporters, marching in disciplined phalanxes, chanting: 'Pakistan ka nara kya hai...La Ilaha Il Ilah.' Though the well-to-do people like Khushwant still moved about and went to their offices and clubs, the trouble was brewing. The Christians had marked out their houses with huge crosses painted in white and the Parsees put up signs saying 'Parsee ka makan.' Khushwant himself escaped being butchered by the mobs. Returning from attending to a case one day, he decided to walk down to catch a train to Lahore. He was surprised to see the road deserted, when a lorry full of Sikh soldiers pulled up and he was ordered to board it. The Sikh officer shouted at him that he must be crazy to be walking out alone, as they had killed all Sikhs in neighbouring villages. He was put on a train and, at Lahore, his friend, Manzur Qadir, received him and shifted him away to safety. Soon after that, Khushwant and his wife decided to leave Lahore.

He had seen violence and bloodshed at close quarters. He recalled the spine chilling episode of encountering a group of Sikh soldiers who boasted that they had killed every man, woman and child in a Muslim village. These images of death and the destruction, of all that was human, remained with him all his life and were immortalised in his novel, *Train to Pakistan*.

Khushwant was never to forget that his Muslim friends in Pakistan had helped him in the Partition days. The closest was Manzur Qadir, who later became his country's Foreign Minister, and who had known him from his early days in Lahore. When Khushwant finally left his house in Lahore, to go to India with his wife, he gave the keys of his house to Manzur Qadir, hoping he would soon return. That was not to be. Manzur then sent all of Khushwant's belongings to India, through friends and travellers. This included half full whiskey bottles from Khushwant's bar in his Lahore house. Quite characteristically, Khushwant mentioned no other belongings but the whiskey bottles in an interview. The bottles were sent to him through a lawyer. 'He drank up the whiskey and I got the empty bottles,' recalled Khushwant.

One-man enquiry into riots

After the riots of 1969 in Gujarat, Khushwant, as he puts it, 'constituted myself into a one-man commission of inquiry,' and toured the state to see things for himself. A web of disinformation and lies, suspicion and supressed hatreds is what he encountered everywhere. The Gujarat riots claimed the lives of nearly 800 Muslims and 260 Hindus, and a total of over 2,000 were injured in an unprecedented scale of carnage.

When he reached Gujarat a few months after the terrible riots, Khushwant spoke to people in both Muslim and Hindu areas, but most of the signs of carnage and arson had been repaired in the months after the riots and nobody wanted to speak the truth. He walked around the bazaars and the once riot affected areas of the city. He tried to talk to the Hindus, but all he heard from them was: 'and you are full of hate.' Writing in his book, *The End of India*, he recalled that from a market, which had been rebuilt after the riots, he hired a scooter belonging to a Muslim. He tried to talk to the driver above the noise of the vehicle and ask him about those terrible days. 'The driver turns around and says, 'You take me for a sucker? I know on which side you are!' Of course, he doesn't say so with his tongue, but with his doleful eyes,' he narrated.

Continuing with his one-man investigation, Khushwant spoke to the shop owners, *paanwallahs* and fruit vendors.

'The result is the same. If they talk, they are Hindus. If they do not, they are Muslims. Both speech and silence are pregnant with hate.' He drove a bit on the outskirts of the city and walked through a graveyard. He found that even the graves and the gravestones hadbeen vandalised. '... my temper mounts and tears come to my eyes,' wrote Khushwant. 'What species of monstrous swine were those who spared neither the places of worship nor the places of the dead?' he lamented. After his tour, he talked to the Mayor of Ahmedabad, who said that it was all over now and 'it will not happen again.' Khushwant returned from there, hoping the Mayor was right, but he himself was not very sure about that.

And, of course, it did happen again and again all over India. He had made this visit after the 1969 riots in Gujarat. Nearly 30 years later, came the arson and the blood chilling Gujarat riots in February 2002. Khushwant was too old at that time to go there and revisit the battlefield of hate and inhumanity. He did say that the 10% Muslim population of Gujarat had been irrevocably alienated by the Sangh wallahs.

The 2002 Gujarat riots followed the Godhra train arson, in which 59 Hindu pilgrims, returning from Ayodhya, were roasted when the train was set on fire and the compartment doors chained and locked. Thirtyone Muslim men were convicted for this train massacre. The riots that followed were a terrible revenge. Khushwant saw the ghost of Partition living through violence and barbarism all over again. He was too involved in the world around him and the state of affairs in this country, unlike the average journalist or a citizen who just did not care and whose usual reaction is one of a sense of tragedy, yet with the mind-set that 'let all these politicians and misguided people do what they want but I will get on with my life as best as I can.' Khushwant reacted using the following wording:

'A wave of anger surges within me and I say to myself... This is my homeland. I will not let these mediaeval minded fundamentalists get away with wasting precious years, squabbling over where exactly a temple should have its foundation stone laid. I will shout my protest from the rooftops.'

He saw in Gujarat that the administration had openly sided with the rampaging mobs of murderers. The attack on the Godhra train had been pre-planned but, instead of putting the perpetrators of that ghastly crime down with a strong hand, the spirit of revenge was fostered. In the carnage that followed, as the Hindus took revenge, hundreds of Muslims were hacked to death, women raped, homes and shops looted and burned down.

His prophetic fears

In 2003, Khushwant wrote that the Sangh wallahs

were not interested in bringing communities together. He commented: 'History will judge them for the damage they have caused but that will happen in the future. Meanwhile, with a triumphant party as their mentor, they will repeat the Gujarat experiment all over India, unless we stop them.' Written nearly a decade before the BJP came to power at the Centre, these words of Khushwant were prophetic; after 2014, new triggers of fanatical violence were added to the armoury of militant Hinduism.

A hitherto unheard of trigger was the spectacle of the beef ban, which led to the formation of belligerent, protection gangs of criminals who call themselves 'gau rakshaks' and went about harassing, beating and even killing people who they accused, usually falsely, of killing cows or eating illegal beef.

Dr Dashrath Gatt, a professor of English at a women's college in Haryana, comments: 'Khushwant Singh insinuates in his writings time and again that it is the majority community, and not the minorities, that poisons the hearts of the common country folk and instigates them, by arousing their communal dislike for people belonging to other communities.' It was a point of view that Khushwant somehow seemed to adhere to in most of his virulent criticism of the rise of Hindu nationalism and there were many who roundly criticised him for this seeming bias in his understanding of the communal situation. His antipathy to the Saffron brand of Hindu belligerence was well known. However he, it is felt, failed to see that much of the communal violence was triggered by the rise of radical Islam, another malevolent force showing itself in the country. Though the Hindus were in the majority, and were now given to intolerance and violence, there were also provocations from the fanatics in the other community. Obviously, in this situation, no one side was absolutely clear if it was entire other side responsible, or the only transgressors.

The first two decades after Independence passed somehow in the tenuous fiction of Nehru secularism, which was heavily accented to be very caring of the minorities. It floundered on the flawed idea of Gandhi that politics must be tempered with the values of religiosity. It was a noble, but perhaps unattainable, idea of a life based on religious values at all levels. But it seemed to have been forgotten that different religions may have values that differed from one another, and that is what caused the conflict. The secularism of Gandhi and Nehru did not mean absence of religion in affairs of state and everyday life; it wanted a tolerant understanding. But in the presence of aggressive religions, there was the possibility of potential conflicts.

Once speaking at a debate on secularism in New Delhi, Khushwant said that Indian secularism was never non-religious. He said: 'There are three or four specific points, which any secular state should have formulated...

No government or political leaders should make a display of their religion, which is common now. The second point is that the state must stop patronising religion. The grant of land for building the places of worship - as seen now by the proliferation of temples and mosques all over the country - is not needed. Third, the misuse of government media, like radio, for broadcasting of religious serials and religion oriented stuff, must be stopped. One can openly see a nauseating misuse of loudspeaker everywhere you go. Take processions, for example...here is another imposition of your religiosity on other people. Muslims, fortunately, only have one procession, the Shias during Muharram. But the Sikhs have ten gurus. So we have their birthdays, days of martyrdom etc. to celebrate.'

Khushwant was convinced that public opinion had to be built up to do all these things. He even criticised telecasting of the *Mahabharata* and the *Ramayana* serials and termed the time spent by people in watching them as 'misused'. 'Let these things be taught in the homes by mothers and parents', was his view, adding, 'To display it for a year on the national television is really an opiate for semiliterate people. It is myth and magic.'

The bold contrarian

When he said things like schools must have no religious instruction or that television must not show the *Ramayana* etc., Khushwant was roundly criticised and called a contrarian.

In fact, M J Akbar did call him that–a man who swam against the tide. Or, at least, he did so as part of his public image, which had made him into a legend. There can be no doubt that the points that Khushwant raised about the omniscience of religion in India, the almost obsessive popularity of myth and blind belief, was something that must be curbed. But his complete denial of religion, especially in a country like India, was like throwing the a baby out with the bathwater. He took an extreme position and extreme positions, though they shock and stir up controversy, seldom lead to constructive change.

To speak against religious fundamentalists engaged in conflict and barbarism, and, therefore, to throw out all religion, was an extreme idea. It was pointed out that science was another body of human knowledge that had also been terribly misused in the past, causing death and suffering. That did not mean science must be eliminated. And it was also true that, in his own personal life, he lived on the twin planks of belief and non-belief. Conflict, cruelty and violence occur even in places like communist countries where there is no religion. India sees conflict and violence over river waters, caste reservations and economic problems. Perhaps he had seen too much of inhumanity and barbarism, and too much of poisonous hate and misery caused by twisted versions of religion, that he was not able to accept that religion could ever be a good thing.

Believed in a personal religion

He was very conscious of the beauty and the sublime ideas that religions had produced; the great Vedic philosophies; the divine songs of Guru Nanak; and the nobility of the Sikh Gurus. He was aware of all the richness of religions but perhaps understood that the masses of people in the world would always misuse religion to justify their lowest impulses. They would be trapped within doctrine and outer symbols of dress, food types and rituals. It was best then, according to Khushwant, to get people away from overdoses of religion, especially in a country like India where religion dominates everyday life, with irrational and sectarian belief. And he believed in what Bertrand Russel had said: 'Every intelligent person must evolve his own personal religion.' It was something Khushwant had certainly done for himself.

Warming to his out-of-the-box ideas, to curb common religion and bring in true secularism, he also spoke strongly in favour of promoting the rational and the scientific temperament. 'You must stop and circumscribe religion, except for the legitimate purpose for which it was originally invented,' said Khushwant. Asked about Advani saying 'it was because of the Hindus that India could be a secular state', he also said that he was willing to concede that if the Muslims had been the same number as the Hindus, they would have declared India an Islamic state. 'We have allowed religion to go absolutely berserk,' opined Khushwant.

Perhaps the worst of the communal barbarism was the 1984 pogrom against the Sikhs, in which nearly 10,000 Sikhs were massacred following the assassination of Mrs Gandhi. Khushwant was broken by the Operation Blue Star attack on the Golden Temple, and its repercussions leading to the assassination of Mrs Gandhi and finally the massacre of the Sikhs that were reportedly led in many cases by Congress leaders. It was not just the Saffron parties, but Nehru's and Gandhi's Congress party that had backed the communal horror. His relations with the Congress party snapped for ever, as he had already returned his Padma Bhushan award after Operation Blue Star. He saw Sikhs near his home being attacked while policemen watched and did nothing to prevent those attacks. He had to be warned and was forced to stay inside his house, and not put himself in danger by going out on the street. Finally, he had to take refuge in Swedish Embassy to save himself. He wrote that he had become a refugee in his own country. Later, he deposed bravely and boldly before the enquiry commissions, despite all allegations against him being totally useless. 'Commissions of injustice' is what he called them.

Though Khushwant was always guided by liberal and humanitarian values, and his love for free thinking, that rejected all doctrine, he confessed many a time to having a special concern for the Muslim minorities who, he thought, were lagging behind and were disadvantaged. It was something he was roundly criticised for, but this went beyond rational evaluation of communalism and its causes.

Khushwant had always believed that geographically, at least, and due to his early years in the western part of an undivided India, his roots were in what was now known as Pakistan. His closest friends lived there. Also, like many Punjabis of that generation, he had an affinity for the Urdu and Muslim culture. Kuldeep Nayar was another such person, who was known to have been working all his life for peace and friendship with Pakistan. He led peace vigils at the Wagah border along with scores of Indian peaceniks, as they were called, who lit candles for invoking Indo-Pakistan amity. Khushwant never did light those candles, but he was close to his Muslim friends and greatly encouraged young Muslims. In no way this diminished his virulent condemnation of Muslim bigots, or his clarity about the force of Muslim fanaticism, which he thought was on par with the fanaticism of Hindus and Sikhs. He had often said that he had no illusions about the power of the mad mobs.

Opposed to regression

In spite of his affinity for Muslim culture, Khushwant was never shy of criticising what he thought was wrong. He was strongly opposed to the Burqa or hijab worn by Muslim women. He was convinced that it was evidence of male suppression and one of the main reasons for keeping the women, and their children and families, in backwardness and illiteracy. This did not make him very popular with the Muslims. Ironically, it was a group of Muslim women who once rebelled against him and said that he had no business in interfering in their choice of dress. Reacting to his statement that 'the Niqab is the single most reprehensible cause for keeping Muslims backward...The sooner it is abolished, the better', Muslim women felt that he should keep his views to himself. They supported the conservative views of Islam that have been espoused and broadcast by a traditionalist Islamic leader, Zakir Naik, whom Khushwant met once at a book fair.

He said he found the Muslim radical leader's pronouncements somewhat juvenile. In his words: 'I disagree with almost everything he has to say...Though by definition (a kaffir), I don't believe in God, Satan, angels, heaven or hell. I feel hurt and angry because I am emotionally and rationally bothered by the sorry plight of Muslims today.'

He asked Naik why eating pig meat is forbidden in Islam. Naik's answer was that a pig not only eats garbage, including human and animal excreta, The pig is the most shameless animal on the face of the earth. It is the only animal that invites its friends to have sex with its mate. Khushwant had a good laugh at this and said that he was not aware of this 'aberration.'

In the end, after Naik had finished his diatribe against

alcohol, women's liberation and the western society, and also extolled the virtues of polygamy, Khushwant concluded: 'All I can say in reply is, Dr Naik, you know next to nothing about the western society and you are talking through your skull cap. People like you are making the Muslims lag behind other communities.'

He dismissed Naik in those few words. In the years after Khushwant's death, Zakir Naik gained a phenomenal popularity with his Islamic religious TV channel and the government, at last, is currently investigating the sources of his funds that have been used for his radical propaganda, which have further led to the ghettoisation of the most backward and the illiterate among the Muslims.

Meeting Guru Golwalkar

The pattern is repeated in other communities where the semiliterate and the economically weaker people, those who need peace and prosperity the most, are persuaded by rabble rousing fanatics to forget everything else except the hate and anger that somehow gives them a reason for living. In his quest to understand the spread of bigotry that has made a section of Indians one of the most brutal people on the earth, Khushwant also met the then RSS chief, Guru Golwalkar. Khushwant was tireless and painstaking in his pursuit to meet such people on a one-to-one basis and to understand what drove them to motivate people in such negative ways.

He confessed in his write-up on the RSS leader that he had been at the top of his hit list because: 'I could not forget the RSS in communal riots, the assassination of the Mahatma, and the talk of changing India, from a secular to a Hindu state. However, as a journalist, I could not resist the chance of meeting him.' He found Guru Golwalkar a physically frail man, in his mid-60s, with a fixed smile on his face. At the outset, Golwalkar said that there was no militarism in his movement and added: 'We value discipline and that is another matter.'

To his question about the RSS attitude towards the minorities, Golwalkar said RSS had nothing against them. 'A delegation of the Muslims came to see me. I told them that Muslims must forget that they ruled India. They should not look upon foreign Muslim countries as their homeland. They must join the mainstream of Indian-ism,' Golwalkar said.

Khushwant then asked him why he pinned his faith on religion, when most of the world was turning anti-religious and agnostic. The answer was that Hinduism was on a firm ground because it had no dogma. 'It had been challenged by agnostics before; it will survive the wave of irreligiousness... Agnosticism will overtake them (Christianity and Islam), but it will not overtake Hinduism. Ours is not a religion in the dictionary sense of the word; it is a way of life. Hinduism will take care of agnosticism.'

Khushwant admitted that he was impressed with the

meeting, as the RSS leader gave him the impression that he was open to persuasion. He accepted Golwalkar's invitation to visit him at the RSS headquarters. 'Maybe I can bring him around to make the Hindu-Muslim unity as the main aim of the RSS. Or, am I being a simple minded Sardarji?' Khushwant thought.

It was his tireless but a determined quest to meet people, to understand, and perhaps to persuade them out of their habits of dogmatic thought. As Khushwant was to find out time and time again, people take up positions and build up passions about them to such an extent that they cannot go back on the fanaticism they have induced upon themselves. Occasionally, he also fell out with some friends because of these matters. This happened with a once close friend, Arun Shourie, the Magsaysay award winner and a former editor of *The Indian Express* and the *Hindustan Times*. Khushwant had been a frequent diner in Shourie's household. At one dinner party there, among the other guests was also Kuldeep Nayar. The conversation was largely about Advani's *Rath Yatra* in 1990. Khushwant said that he had no doubt that the whole exercise had been undertaken with the intent to destroy the Babri masjid. To this, Shourie commented, 'Who says it is a mosque?' Khushwant was taken aback. He asked Shorey if he had ever seen a building, with three domes and a wall facing Mecca, which is not a mosque. Shourie did not reply. Later, Khushwant admitted: 'Since then, we have been on opposite sides; he on the mosque breakers'. I wanted them (mosque breakers) to be arrested and punished for the criminal act of vandalism...I stopped associating with Arun Shourie.'

As Khushwant was to find, the debate on communalism has many arguments, doctrinaire thinking, and justification on all sides. As long as habits of thought and chauvinistic attitude are kept in a state of unmoving stubbornness, there can bc no final solution. It is also true that, in spite of all the arguments, there is only one way to look at communalism -with condemnation. Khushwant did this in everything that he wrote on the subject. He also, as we have seen, lost no opportunity to see things for himself and to meet the people who were the chief players in this endless drama of justifying the unjustifiable and taking sacrosanct positions at the cost of human lives and violence.

Naipaul and Khushwant

Khushwant met the noted writer, VS Naipaul, whom he admired and was very friendly with him, whenever the Noble laureate visited India. Brought together once for a discussion, the two writers came round to talking about Naipaul's book, *Beyond Belief*, in which he writes at length about Islam. Naipaul maintained Islam is an Arab religion and said, 'Everyone who is not an Arab is a convert. Islam is a demanding religion and a convert to Islam changes his view of the world. His holy places are in another country, his secret language is Arabic. He rejects his own history and turns away from his own historical background. In a profound way, the converted Muslims are a colonised people.'

Khushwant thought that Naipaul was disenchanted with Islam. Naipaul denied this, claiming he was being a realist, and added, 'The fundamentalists in places like Malaysia and Indonesia want to get rid of everything that reminds them of their non-Muslim past. This is also true of Iran. Persia was a great country. It rivalled the Roman Empire… challenged classical Greece. Now they are saying that the pre-Islamic period is not important. There had been an attempt in Iran to destroy the ruins of Persepolis and the remnants of Cyprus Palace, built 2,500 years ago... This is the direction fanaticism will take people in. One has to compare that with other societies where the past is cherished and endlessly explored.'

Naipaul then asked Khushwant about the rise of Hindu nationalism. 'It distresses me,' said Khushwant, adding,'There has been a rise in intolerance towards everything that is not Hindu and it is gaining momentum.' Giving the example of the vandalism against the painter, M F Husain, who had painted a Hindu goddess in the nude, Khushwant said it would not have happened if the artist had been a Hindu. 'You can walk into any antique shop and pick up a carving of Shiva and Parvati coupling. There are many paintings of Radha and Krishna making love in the most graphic manner,' he told Naipaul, who replied, 'the Hindu fundamentalists are mimicking the Islamic fundamentalists.'

Khushwant was surprised when Naipaul said, 'The destruction of the Babri masjid was 'an act of historical balancing'. The mosque built by Babar was meant as an act of contempt. Babar was no lover of India. I think it is universally accepted that Babar despised India, the Indian people and their fate.' Khushwant said he thought a new beginning would have been made in 1947 and the past would be left to the past and added, 'This kind of insanity will spell disaster for the country.'

Moving aside from the dreary subject, Naipaul asked Khushwant, 'Tell me about love; what aspect of love interests you?' Khushwant did not take a moment to give his reply: 'The earthy aspect, the physical aspect, the lusty aspect, all aspects of love…I do understand lust but, as hard as I try, I can't understand the concept of love.'

To this, Naipaul remarked, 'People who are not sexually fulfilled are hard people and extraordinarily damaged... Lots of sexual repression comes out in the form of violence. A lot of religious intolerance is a product of sexual frustration.' To which Khushwant had his own comment, 'I said to LK Advani once, 'You are a good and honest man. But you don't drink, you don't smoke and you don't womanise. Such men are dangerous!'

The only glimmer of hope that Khushwant saw towards

the end of his life, in this matter of spreading communal hatred and hardening of attitudes amongst the fanatics of all religions, was in the young. He thought that the young people were now better educated and wanted more out of life than the traditionalists and the conservatives.

Khushwant had seen communalism and its violence at close quarters all his life. He had travelled through the dark tunnel to try to find a light at the end of it. His hope in the young of India was the only light that he could see. It can only be partially true. For, as much as there are young Indians of all religions, who are forging ahead with higher education and ambitions of professionalism and a good life, many of them turning away from the doctrinaire aspects of religions; there are also young people, mostly in the underprivileged sections of society, who are moving more and more towards fanaticism. These people, who are without employment and are semi-literate, are becoming Hindutva vigilantes or Islamic radicals, many of them joining the dreaded ISIS. Being a historian, however, he believed that history has its own force and logic. 'Unless a miracle saves us,' he wrote, 'the country will break up. It will not be Pakistan or any other foreign power that will destroy us; we will commit hara-kiri.'

His own kind of religion

The dangers of religion

Men of intelligence in every age have condemned the misuse of religion by evil men. They have known that all the atrocities, and the untold cruelty and oppression, which have been visited upon the innocents of the world, had nothing to do with the essentially humane and noble teachings of religions. And yet, neither religion nor, as we see in modern times, science can ever be free from the evil that rules the minds of men. It comes as no the famous that cosmologist, Stephen Hawking, has now said that; somewhere in the future, science will become, as religion has already done, the greatest danger to mankind.

Khushwant had seen the worst of bloodshed and

barbarism that men trapped in the fanaticism of their religious beliefs are capable of. He had spent his early years in the western part of Punjab, which later became a part of Pakistan, and went through the trauma of the Partition. After witnessing everything that had happened around him during the Partition, he once said that he thought it was the end of his country. It was certainly the end of an era for India, which would henceforth be continually ravaged by the communal dragon. He saw men with blood on their hands gloating and celebrating over the fact that they had killed women and children of another community. He walked through the ravaged streets of embattled cities, where he saw, heard and felt the hate and rage that transforms ordinary peaceful people into veritable demons. He did not have to go anywhere or see any of this, but an essential and deep-rooted humanity made him leave his house and go to riot affected areas. Writing about it was only one part of what he had in mind. He had to, he felt, understand this and go deeper into the reasons why these things happen. It is what all men of thought and compassion have tried to do in their lifetimes—to be involved, feel the suffering, and try to know the reasons for it.

And like many men before him, Khushwant began to be convinced in his mind that it was religion, actually all the different kinds of religions that men follow, that was the reason for this strange and terrible transformation of men into violent, inhuman fanatics. As a witness to the time in which he lived, Khushwant was deeply involved in reporting, understanding and trying to be a philosopher, and guide the people. He denied and criticised religion, and yet he knew more about it; he had read, discussed and deliberated more on religion then most men and women do. He had translated religious poems and scriptures of many religions, for they were all the same to him. He had read the Upanishads and the Hindu religious texts, he had studied and translated the scriptures of his own Sikh religion, he had gone deep into the verses of the Koran, and had at various times familiarised himself with Buddhism, Jainism, Zoroastrianism and other faiths.

And he was to say: 'It is evident that all religious systems have failed us. They have generated more misunderstanding and hatred than love and friendship. However, since some people need some sort of system of beliefs, we have to evolve a new religion that avoids the pitfalls of outworn creeds of which we have had a better experience…The process has to be dual: first, wipe the slate clean and then start afresh to write a new message.'

This was a theme that Khushwant was to write about almost on every occasion that the subject came up. And yet, his repeated emphasis on the need for a new religion was most probably only his way of saying that what had been wrought by the older religions was expendable. He was too wise and erudite, in the ways of history and humankind, to think that any new religion could really solve the problem of hate and brutality in man. He was very aware of the great beauty, wisdom, and nobility that the religions had also created. He often said, purely as a man of literature, that he often read the Old Testament, the verses of the Koran and the Gita for their literary excellence. In fact, his books, *Religion and Agnostic Khushwant—There is no God'*, in which he put forth his arguments against religion and asked for a new religion, are actually full of quotations and verses from the scriptural books of the various religions.

A personal God

Khushwant certainly had a complex and a very personal relationship with religion. And though he denied the existence of God, one could also say that he had his own kind of relationship with his own kind of god. He rejected the idea of a humanoid, personal God, but acknowledged there are other perceptions of the mystery that surrounds us. He was looking for it all his life.

Though he had often called himself an agnostic, it is possible that when he put the words 'There is no God' on the cover of a book, it was more at the nudging of populism; for agnosticism is not as interesting as atheism. However that may be, it was his manner and his style to say things for emphasis.

He begins his book, *Religion*, with the following words:

'Have you seen God? No, I have not. Nor do I believe that anyone, at any time, past or present, has seen him. As for me, even if I come face-to-face with him, I would not recognise him. Were he to give me his visiting card and say, 'I am God', I would say in utter disbelief, 'Tell me another."

It was his way of being able to reduce the supposedly sublime to the ridiculous. It was the way of a man who had learnt to laugh at everything, even the most ponderous and serious of matters. It is the way in which a man of intelligence usually finds freedom from doctrine and the pitfalls of over seriousness, by deconstructing the self-righteous and the self-important. As we go along these pages, we shall see Khushwant denied the gods of the religions, the ideas and images that men had formed and which they fought over, but he had certainly evolved some kind of religion of his own. Though it was not defined even to him, and though he kept talking wistfully of a 'new religion', he was a man who lived by his own kind of faith in the things that resonated in his nature and his being. MJ Akbar has said: 'He pretended he did not believe in God. But God certainly believed in him.'

In the course of his wide reading, Khushwant had tried to follow the ideas of other men who had travelled the path of atheism, though he himself was only a partial nonbeliever. We shall go into that in a moment. One such self-declared atheist was the writer and playwright, George Bernard Shaw, another creative thinker who satirised social hypocrisy and stultifying morals. Shaw had never believed in the accepted faith of any specific religious organisation and had made no secret of it. He had called himself an atheist until he was thirty or so. He became one, he later quipped, before he could think. He described the doctrines of the Church of Ireland, which he attended as a child, as unintelligible or 'absurd'. Khushwant quotd Shaw: 'Every intelligent man must create his own religion.'

In his book, *The New Theology*, Shaw has said: 'When you are asked, 'Where is God, who is God?', stand up and say, "I am God and here is God, not as yet completed but still advancing towards completion just in so much as I am working for the purpose of the universe…"' In his later years, he was to develop his own understanding of life and existence. He came to believe in some mystical, poorly defined yet clearly envisioned, life force realising itself through nature and evolution. It appears that Shaw's belief in a life force was as much faith-based as traditional religion, which he opposed all his life. One can quite easily see a parallel here with Khushwant's thinking.

In fact, at a time when he was in London, and decided to make a break with bureaucratic jobs and a career in diplomacy, the first thing Khushwant did was to go to his own Sikh identity and his religion. He made a translation of the Sikh scripture, the *Japji Sahib*. It was to set a pattern for his future work on Sikhism. He not only went on to write the much acclaimed *A History of Sikhs,* he also made translations of verses from the *Guru Granth Sahib* and gave lectures on Sikhism at various British and American universities. He kept his disbelief, or one may call it a dormant atheism, quite effectively on another shelf.

Khushwant's one-time protégée, MJ Akbar, was to write in the *Guardian:* 'Absence of faith (for Khushwant) did not mean absence of belief…The agnostic in Khushwant surrendered easily, and I think willingly, to the touch of the divine.'

This comes to mind because Khushwant himself had once written: 'Many a time in Tokyo, when I got up at three in the morning to work on translations of the hymns of Guru Nanak, I felt the hand of the Guru on my shoulder. Though I knew it was make-believe, I found it comforting.' Akbar takes a courageous view and wonders whether he really did consider it to be 'make-belief.' He says: 'I doubt it. Khushwant Singh would have never have found comfort in the false.'

Philosophies of doubt and discovery

Interestingly, one reads of some other great writers and thinkers who have had the same kind of reactions to the faults of the religions. Even though we know that every religion was born out of the visionary ideas and the wisdom of highly evolved men, all faiths were quickly corrupted. We think of the existentialist philosopher and writer, Jean Paul Sartre, who wrote during and after the Second World War. Sartre told the world: 'Man is alone and is condemned to be free…he is responsible for whatever he does and whatever he is.' He told a post-war generation that, in the absence of God, man was on his own and it was up to him what he did to himself or to others – Existentialism. It was a stark and realistic philosophy that struck at the very root of established Christianity and other religions. And yet, Sartre was also to say: 'That God does not exist, I cannot deny. That my whole being cries out for God, I cannot forget.' And it happened that, on his dying bed, Sartre seem to have reneged from his entire life's philosophy of the existentialist denial of God. This astonishing change was revealed by his friend and ex-Maoist, Benny Levy, who spent much of his time with the dying Sartre. According to him, he had a drastic change of mind about the existence of God and started gravitating toward messianic Judaism.

Sartre had said: 'I do not feel that I am the product of chance, a speck of dust in the universe, but someone who was expected, prepared, prefigured. In short, a being whom only a creator could put here; and this idea of a creating hand refers to God.' His lifetime friend and lover, Simone de Beauvoir, herself an acclaimed thinker and writer, attended his funeral as his widow (though they were never married and believed in free love) but after the funeral, she castigated him bitterly for his changing the philosophy of a lifetime, a philosophy which millions of the post-war generation had blindly followed when Sartre had told them that there was no God and that 'they must learn to live alone.'

When asked, and this was to happen quite often, as to the ambivalence in his attitude to religion and God, in the sense that he was so deeply preoccupied with both while he denied them, Khushwant was neither discomfited nor ever felt the need to explain. He perhaps felt that there really was no need to fit into a stereotype definition of being this or that. The word 'agnostic' was vague enough, but good enough. And he was so right about this because most often we get trapped by our own or by others' definitions. In fact, it is interesting to note that the people, who believe in religions and are fanatical about them, spend a lot of time and energy in imposing their views upon everyone else. In extreme cases, this also takes the form of proselytising and conversion. But the people who criticise them for their fanaticism and their drive to impose their religion on others, these people—the non-believers and the atheists—also seem to be in the same trap. They go to great lengths to prove that atheism and a world without God is the only truth. Both seem to overlook the fact that, in all discussion about the good or the bad of religion, the comparisons of symbols, beliefs, and taboos have nothing to do with the central idea of God, which is universal and exists in many forms.

In fact, it may well be said that Khushwant was among those people who may not have believed in a religious God, but he had used his essential nature and thought processes, to find his own spiritual roots, his own vision of life, in a multiplicity of ideas and things, experiences and people, other cultures and belief systems. Life in all its diversity resonated in him with its newness and its endless possibilities and, as a man of sensitivity and intellect, he felt it all himself. And yet, this deeply serious man found a way, as do many spiritual people, to bring this all into him with a touch of lightness, the laughter of the wise. There is very little in almost any religion for individualism and personal belief. The rebel, who does not accept what is laid down by the priest, has no place in the religious environment. Khushwant had noted often in his writings that severity and fear, the necessity to obey and the importance of total surrender to an all-knowing, all just and powerful God, who was judging humans at all times was the hallmark of the Abrahamic religions, which included Christianity, Islam and Judaism. In the Hinduism group of religions, spanning Jainism, Buddhism and Sikhism, the emphasis was on prayer, devotion to a supreme Divinity that controlled life and destiny and man, in a sense, could do nothing about it. 'My judgement is that there is no basis for believing either,' he was to say.

According to him, if one system believes in a Day of Judgement, when all the souls of the dead will rise to have their lives assessed by the Creator for everlasting reward or punishment, then 'the queue must be miles long', which he dismissed. 'The Hindu belief in reincarnation sounds more sophisticated,' he said, but concluded, there is nothing in it.' It was the reaction of a thoughtful man in a very simplistic manner to all that he had seen in the world, the hate and the killings, the humbug of sham morality, piousness and the injustice that was continuously heaped upon people by the taboos and the diktats of religion. As we are to see again and again in his work and thinking, he was drawn to the various aspects of religion that were creative and positive. But what men had done to the religions led him to conclude that they had done more harm than good to men.

'If you look at things as they are, there does not seem to be a code, either of man or of God, on which one can turn one's conduct,' he wrote in his novel, *Train To Pakistan*. 'Wrong triumphs over right, as much as right over wrong, sometimes its tramps are greater… In such circumstances, what can you do but cultivate an utter indifference to all values?'

It was his strong belief that the important thing was to develop and practice your own values, according to your own intelligence. In any case, when social norms and values were different in different societies, it was obvious that there were no absolute values; right action was a relative matter and all the values given by religions were followed more in the breach than in the practice. Human nature was always going to be a factor in the practice of religion and there was always going to be a conflict because of the weaknesses of the human nature. He had portrayed much of this in his novels and short stories, the insidious workings of life and circumstances that forced people to become what they were, to act as they did. Giving the example of ancient Indian systems that question the existence of God, he had concluded that conduct was more important than belief and criticised the fact that, 'our religious thinkers asserted that not only did God exist, but questioning his existence amounted to blasphemy.'

He was to often quote one of the greatest atheists, Bertrand Russell, who had advanced the most cogent arguments against organised religion. 'Religion', wrote Russell, 'is something left over from the infancy of our intelligence; it will fade away as we adopt reason and science as our guidelines.' Of course, this was not to happen in the nearly half a century since the passing away of that great atheist. The more somethings are wronged sometimes, the more they persist in the human experience because they seem to fulfil a paradoxical need for the good as well as the evil. The Hindu practice of caste, obnoxious as it is and unjust, is one of these things, which at one time fulfilled a social need and went on to fulfil a mendacious and evil need for superiority and cruelty to fellow humans. The truth of the matter is that religion is also one such system and people like Bertrand Russell could never wish it away. Khushwant had gone often to Bertrand Russell and George Bernard Shaw for ideas on these matters and though, as we have said, much of his interest revolved around God and religion, he agreed with their ideas. Russell had once written:

'Religion prevents our children from having a rational education; religion prevents us from removing the fundamental causes of war; and religion prevents us from teaching the ethics of scientific cooperation in place of the old fears and doctrine of sin and punishment. It is possible that mankind is on the threshold of a golden age, but if so, it will be necessary first to slay the dragon that guards the door. And this dragon is religion. There is an echo of these ideas in Khushwant, who is also known to have said that there must be a stop to building temples, schools must be set up instead and that there is a need for the scientific temper and for practising the work ethic instead of wasting time in prayer and ritual.

The strong, often vehement, belief of the atheist believer in God, as well as the denial of god by the atheist, were both exaggerations and Khushwant was to see this quite clearly with his simple common sense wisdom. He was to say often that it was of little consequence whether God existed or not. Agnostic or atheist, the two terms used by him in books, were in actual fact his natural sense of freedom, as he did not accept even those boundaries. Much of his work of translating the hymns of the Sikh Gurus, as also his painstakingly done English rendering of Allama Iqbal's epic poems, *Shikwa and Jawab-e-Shikwa,* which were addressed to Allah, dealt with God and divinity. That would have put off any hardened atheist, who would have found the spiritual fantasy and the holy and devout imagery disagreeable. It was never so with Khushwant, who kept himself open to the beauty of thought in the poetry.

A lover's quarrel with God

Khushwant was a creative and sensitive man, who responded to the flights of thought in religious poetry. At such times, the non-believer seemed to disappear. Even the iconoclasts like Mirza Ghalib, his much loved poet, had dipped their pens in a rich sarcasm and a lover's quarrel with God. They complained, jested and even ridiculed the injustice and waywardness of God. It was not a denial. The denial was of the priests and mullahs, the straitjacket of taboos and doctrine, and the mindless importance given to ritual and mechanical mantras, and telling of beads. Khushwant had read of Guru Nanak and of Ghalib on a theme that was similar and which showed the pervasive freedom of their vision of divinity. In the story of Guru

Nanak, which Khushwant repeated, the founder of Sikhism was sitting with his legs turned towards Mecca. He was asked to move his legs away from that direction. Guru Nanak asked those who had objected how to turn his feet to any direction where God was not present. The poet, Ghalib (Khushwant in his later years called him 'my companion), loved his drinks, and, like Khushwant, was partial to Scotch whiskey, which he procured from British officers. Ghalib, echoing the awareness of the omniscience of God, wrote:

Zahid sharab peene de masjid mein baith kar;
Ya woh jagah bataa jahaan khudaa na ho.
(Or let me sit here in the masjid and drink wine;
Or tell me a place where there is no God).

It was the spirituality and the lightness, the world-weary wisdom of all life and the disenchantment with enforced religiosity, the hallmarks of the freethinker or the mystic that appealed to Khushwant. What was important was life itself and the ways that men lived it. All else, the promises of an afterlife, the hypocrisy of committing sin and cruelty, and then going to priests and pundits to find expiation for their deeds or thronging the banks of rivers, as the Hindus did, to wash away their sins, was sheer nonsense. He was very clear about this. And he often quoted Guru Nanak on the matter; 'You may be at the sixty-eighth places of pilgrimage, it will not wash the dirt off your body (and mind).' Yet it does not deter the Guru's followers from doing precisely what he had told them were useless practices, or from going to pilgrim centres. Millions of Hindus turn up to bathe and wash away their sins at the Ganges and other holy rivers all the year round. Probably, the largest congregations of humans in the world is held at the Kumbh Mela at the confluence of the Ganges and the Yamuna at Triveni, near Allahabad. Instead of the emphasis being on living with a sense of goodness and right behaviour, the emphasis is on an outer practice of taking a bath, which has nothing to do with purifying the mind, according to Khushwant.

It was his observation of such incongruous practices in religion, the stubborn adherence to ritual and symbolic actions, thought to be of spiritual merit, that he criticised. There were also questions of human suffering, the eternal problem of pain in the presence of a supposedly benign God, the accidents that happen to people who go on pilgrimages, the suffering of the innocent and of children who have done no wrong, that bothered him. He often quoted these lines from the philosopher, Epicurus:.

Is God willing to prevent evil but not able?
Then he is not omnipotent
Is he able but not willing? Then he is malevolent.
Is he both able and willing? Then whence cometh evil?
Is he neither able nor willing? Then why call him God.

And almost in a kind of existential despair, Khushwant wrote: 'No my friends, there is no justice in the world. To succeed in life you have to be the three Cs... *chalak, chaploos* and *char-sau-bees* (cunning, sycophant and a cheat, as defined under Section 420 of the IPC).'

In this respect, he had some praise for the followers of the Jain faith, for he noted that they have no place for God in their theology. Instead, the Jains believe in enlightened human beings and in good conduct. They also reject the Vedas, the priestly order of the Brahmins and the caste system. He goes on to talk about the futility of believing in miracles and gives the example of a film, *Nanak Naam Jahaaz*, in which millions of people saw a blind man visiting gurdwaras all over India and finally had his vision restored. People who saw this movie, he says, 'were convinced that it was the truth, when in their hearts they knew it was a lie.' Religions also promote all kinds of fads about food and not eating cows or pigs, the ways in which they are to be slaughtered, and the other fads of vegetarians, some of whom do not eat things that grow under the earth for fear of destroying insects and worms that cling to them; all these were unnecessary and totally extraneous to any kind of spiritual endeavour. Most of these taboos can be easily explained as belonging to a certain time and social environment.

In his unforgettable book, *Cows, Pigs, Wars and Witches—The Riddles of Culture,* author Marvin Harris wrote with great perception about these taboos that infest our religions.

He pointed out that the cow became a holy animal for the Hindus because it was economically a very valuable asset to the Hindu society, as it was capable of converting grass into protein needed for human growth. Indiscriminate killing of cows for food would have decimated their numbers drastically and so the elders in society put a ban on eating beef. He explained the almost fanatical dread and sinfulness involved in eating pig among the Muslims, as easily. The pig, according to Harris, is an animal that does not have breathing pores on its skin and, therefore, needs water or moisture to cool its body all the time. The pig in most ancient societies, especially in the dry desert areas, began to wallow in dirt, urine and excrement because it had to cool itself and, thus, became the carrier of dreaded diseases. It was, therefore, banned as a dirty animal. However, modern piggery, everywhere today, has the most hygienic conditions, in which pigs are reared and there is no reason at all for considering them as dirty. The witches too have been a constant in religions; millions of women were burnt alive in the Christian inquisitions and the Muslims, with the Hindus not being too far behind. In most cases, these unfortunate women, and also men considered to be possessed by the devil, were people who questioned the diktats of the religions to which they belonged. They were a threat to the authority of the church. In many cases, many of them recorded in India, women have been killed or done away with by their own families, who denounced them as witches for the simple reason that their properties had to be grabbed.

Some wishful thinking on the new religion

'Evolving a personal religion for myself has been a lifelong quest', Khushwant has said, whilst quoting the poet Iqbal:

> *'Oh Iqbal, I go about everywhere looking for myself,*
> *As if I were the wayfarer, as well as the destination.'*

Understanding that religion can be, and has always been, a very strong and often misused organising force in any society and, therefore, Khushwant in his books, *Religion and Agnostic Khushwant,* goes on to do some very logical wishful thinking on the need for a new religion. As a man of the world, and one who had seen the great depths of influence that the religions wield upon the common people, it seems unlikely that he ever thought that his wish list for the new religion would ever come into being or be popularly accepted. However, what he had to say about the new religion is interesting: 'If only as an intelligent man's guidelines to thinking people, of whom there are more in the silent majority than we care to believe, to fashion a way of living for themselves and their families.'

The first thing that he underlined is that the new religion must be based on the work ethics. In a country where every religion has its holidays, days of fasting, festivals, and birthdays and death anniversaries of its holy men, all of which are spent in feasting or sheer indolence, he said that we have a very apt motto in India, which needs to be put into effect: '*aaraam haraam hai* (inactivity / inaction / indolence is forbidden).' He goes on to say that India must reject the concept of 'sanyas,' (leaving or relinquishing the world). According to him, Guru Nanak emphasised the work ethic in three commandments: *kirt karo* (do work), *naam japo* (take the name or worship) and *vand chakho* (give to charity). Those who do not contribute materially to society have no right to claim any benefits from it. In a country where there are millions of ascetics, wandering holy men, sadhus and non-working people living in ashrams and religious orders, Khushwant's exhortation that they must all work is a radical suggestion. Most of these holy men are actually either drop-outs by themselves or people who could never get any employment or work of any kind. He also comes down heavily on people from what he called 'useless professions.' These include astrologers, palmists, crystal ball gazers, and those engaged in deciphering astrological ancient texts like the *Bhrigu Samhita* and the *Lal Kitaab*, as also other mythical books, which claim to foretell the future of every human being on earth. He called for a ban on all these, as well as the *pujas, mahurats* and performances of *yagnas* etc. by political leaders and top industrialists.

He was particularly harsh on astrology, which he said has got religious sanction and, therefore, must be exorcised from the new religion. He wrote: 'That it (astrology) is totally unscientific is beyond dispute. Astronomy is a science; astrology is not. What superstition is to religion, astrology is to astronomy...the illegitimate offspring of sick minds.' He pointed out at instances in history where kings and commanders did not use their own common sense and strategy planning but consulted astrologers as to the place and method of attack. The stars invariably forfeited their destinies. The same goes for marriage, in which astrology is considered of great importance in India. There is, however, no evidence at all that astrologically good or auspicious marriages do any better than others. The divorce rate in India has been steadily going up in modern times. He spoke about population control and the preservation of environment. In his new religion, he gave the example of the Bishnoi community of Rajasthan, perhaps the earliest true environmentalists, who believe that all life is sacred and became famous some years ago for the 'Chipko' movement against the felling of trees.

Bold, as only he could be, he said in this regard that the cremation of Hindus and Sikhs on funeral pyres of wood must be stopped, as it is a waste of wood. He seemed to advocate burial as an alternative and, approvingly, cited the example of Hindu communities in South India who bury their dead. Chief Ministers, such as CN Annadurai and MG Ramachandran, were buried. Many monks and holy men are also given a burial. And with his penchant for factual information, he said that the amount of wood consumed in cremation is horrendous.

'More than one crore Indians die every year, of whom 80 per cent are Hindus or Sikhs. Two quintals of wood are consumed in cremating one dead body, making a staggering total of millions of quintals of wood consumed every year. We are destroying our forests to dispose of our dead... Humans, when they die, should be returned to the earth from which, according to most religions, they emanate', Khushwant maintained.

Once he got started, there was no stopping Khushwant: 'I would treat religious scriptures as historical writings... They should not become subject matter of prayer. Places of worship should be converted to schools, colleges or hospitals or simply preserved as historical monuments.'

Quite unlike him, he also made a strong plea for vegetarianism, giving the Jain ideal of nonviolence as an example. Instead of prayer and chanting mantras, he suggested that people should set aside an hour of the day for social service:

'And finally before retiring for the night, everyone should spend at least fifteen minutes in tune with himself or herself...Look squarely into the reflection of your own eyes and ask yourself, 'Did I hurt anyone today? If so, I must make amends tomorrow'...It is not very easy to face one's own conscience, but it is the ultimate test that one must pass', he recommended and quoted Shakespeare:

This above all: to thine own self be true
And it must follow as the night the day
Thou canst not then be false to any man

It was a creed he lived by. The ultimate individualist, who did not look for, nor always got approval for, his bravery of thought and his courage to swim against the tide when the tide was going the wrong way. And though he had once, perhaps on the spur of the moment, been critical of the literary merit of Tagore, he was to say later that he followed the great exhortation of the Nobel laureate: 'Ekla Chalo Re...' (If no one comes to walk with you, then you must walk alone).

Zorba the Sardar

Among gurus and spiritualists

As we have seen, the denial of religion and the doubt about God did not mean that Khushwant had turned away from them. On the contrary, the existence of his doubt, based on what men had done with religion and God all through the centuries, led him to go deeper and deeper into the philosophies, the Scriptures and the people who were behind all this. As he often said, there were good people and there were frauds. He once noted that it was strange that, in almost all religions, one could doubt the existence of God but one could not doubt the prophets or anything said about them. It was his view that the prophets, like the avatars, saints and messiahs, were great and good human beings; therefore, they must be honoured, but not worshipped. It was something that would probably never happen, especially in a country like India, where all kinds of people, from politicians to charlatans, Godmen and even actors and actresses are worshipped.

Khushwant made it a point to make the journey, whenever he could, to the ashrams and organisations of a large number of gurus and Godmen who were hitting the headlines in his time. He went to them with an open mind and always with his prior announcement that he was an agnostic. This usually made them wary, especially in cases where the person in question was unable to deal with a doubting Thomas. Most of these gurus are accustomed to unquestioning devotion and blind belief, and have very little to give in terms of explanations and arguments, except for the usual platitudes and clichés about divinity and divine knowledge, which only they seem to possess. Khushwant did not believe in any of them of course but was intrigued by the millions of Indians who went to meet these people. During a visit of the Satya Sai Baba to Delhi and soon after, there had been a major controversy about the seemingly miraculous materialisations of various objects, like rings and watches, by the Godman, Khushwant wrote: 'The Indian soil is very productive of prophets and messiahs. We have always had men and women claiming to be incarnations of God, or even God himself in the human form...This sort of belief in men or women being Gods would be regarded as blasphemy by the Christians or get a sentence of death in Islam, yet the Hindu group of religions treat them as holy beings…If anyone is to be put on a shrink's couch, it is not the Godman but his followers…To find out what is missing in their lives which they hope to fulfil by associating with these Godmen.'

Thought highly of Osho

Khushwant, however, persisted in trying to meet as many of the spiritual gurus as he could and also read some of their books and transcripts of talks. This was part of a pattern in his attitude to religion and God. He denied what was wrong and unacceptable to the intelligence, but he still wanted to know what it was all about. He was drawn to the ideas of a maverick spiritual guru, Acharya Rajneesh, known to his disciples as Osho. He wrote about having read Osho's autobiography titled, *Autobiography of A Spiritually Incorrect Mystic*, and also his interest in trying to read everything spoken by Osho, on tape or taken down by his followers and also the innumerable books containing his sermons. On Osho, Khushwant said, 'I do so because I regard him as a proponent of new ideas on existence, its purposes and whatever, if anything, remains of us after death. He was an iconoclast who held nothing sacred, questioned the veracity of religious dogma and cleaned the cobwebs of thinking…' According to Khushwant, and this is a thought that is shared by countless people all over the world, who were not bamboozled by his controversial image, Osho was 'much the most erudite of world's religious philosophers.

He was witty, humorous and often ended his sermons with a dirty joke with four letter words. He was a rare phenomenon.'

Indeed, the controversies raked up about Osho, a totally unconventional spiritual teacher from India from an orthodox Jain family, had made headlines all over the world when he was alive. His emphasis on freedom, both in thought and in action, his even more unabashed encouragement of sexuality and free love, and his total rejection of all religious doctrine had turned him into the enfant terrible of spiritualism in the 80s and 90s. It was rumoured that he had become so powerful and influential in the American society that the US government had tried to poison him with mercury in his food when he was in jail.

Writing about the life of Osho in one of his columns, Khushwant brought out that it was young Rajneesh's mother, though a traditional Jain housewife in a small town, who rejected all customs and encouraged her son to question his teachers, preachers of religion and to think for himself. 'Now I can say,' wrote Osho 'that woman (his mother) was really great, because as far as religion is concerned, everybody is lying. Christians, Jews, Jains, Muslims, everybody is lying. They all talk of God, Heaven and Hell, angels and all kinds of nonsense, without knowing anything at all. She was great not because she knew, but because she was unable to lie to a child.'

Khushwant quoted Osho on the importance of not lying to a child about religion and God, and to let a child find out things for himself / herself: 'Rajneesh thought for himself. He rejected all religions as false…He came to be maligned as a preacher of promiscuity and the sex guru…' Khushwant also said that there are many things, such as the belief in karma and rebirth, that Osho accepted, which Khushwant never did. Osho also promoted the idea of meditation which Khushwant thought was 'a waste of time.'

Osho had started a commune in Pune, which had quickly become a centre of great controversy, because of stories of the practice of free love and tantric sex etc. In that ashram at the height of Osho's popularity, and India was shocked out of its wits. Stories started appearing in the magazines about men and women in the almost altogether, dancing and embracing each other. The lascivious, stunned moral grapevine built up anger and outrage, and ultimately Osho himself was banned from even going to the ashram.

Khushwant narrated the story of a beautiful and sexy Spanish devotee of Osho, who once came to his office at the weekly. She wanted him to meet Osho. The jester that he was, he said his price was that she should sleep with him. Without batting an eyelid, she said that the body was nothing and he could have it, but the soul belonged to Osho. Khushwant was not prepared for such a philosophical rejection and laughed it off. He, however, continued to read Osho. Passages like the following were of great interest to him. Speaking at one of his freewheeling talks, Osho had said: '… Only the son of man is real and only the son of man can grow and become the son of God. Only men can grow and become God, because man is the seed, the source. God is the flowering. God does not exist anywhere. When you flower, God comes into existence. It comes into existence and disappears, comes into existence and disappears. When Buddha was here, God existed. When Jesus was here, God existed... Just as when a flower disappears, it disappears.'

Khushwant's interest and acceptance of the essential ideas of Osho certainly reveals a kindred mind that was not willing to accept any straitjacket thinking at all. This kind of extreme freedom of intellect is bound to alienate a person from the mainstream of conventional thinking and that is what Khushwant lived with, quite happily it must be emphasised, all his life. At a certain point, it even becomes irrelevant whether he believed in God and in which brand of God.

An affectionate and a very fitting tribute was paid to Khushwant in the Osho World Newsletter in April 2014, when a writer, Kul Bhushan, declared him to be 'Zorba the Singh'. He said that Khushwant lived, loved and laughed just like Osho advised everyone to do. 'In Khushwant Singh,' he said, 'we have lost a true Zorba.'

Questions about God

Many great thinkers have lived on the mystical plane of a higher consciousness without believing in the conventional ideas of God. Albert Einstein, for instance, rejected the idea of a God nursemaiding human beings through all the events of their lives and thought it absurd that it was assumed in many traditions that every leaf, every worm and every insect, along with all created beings had a destiny that was monitored day to day by a divine being. Einstein said he was willing to believe in the pantheistic God of Spinoza, who saw the creative forces of nature as a divine principle.

There have been other great scientists, like Max Planck, who did not talk about God but said: 'All matter originates and exists only by virtue of a force…We must assume behind this force the existence of a conscious and intelligent mind. This mind is the matrix of all matter… Having studied the atom, I am telling you that there is no matter as such. All matter arises and persists only due to a force that causes the atomic particles to vibrate, holding them together in the tiniest of solar systems, the atom…Yet, in the whole of the universe, there is no force that is either intelligent or eternal and we must, therefore, assume that behind this force there is a conscious, intelligent mind or spirit. This is the very origin of all matter.'

Khushwant's wide reading and assimilation of ideas of all cultures freed him from the need for definitions and so it was that, in his own way, he believed in things that he could see and understand and feel. He believed in an essential humanity, the possibility of freedom and wisdom without barriers, and also in the need for kindness. 'So many gods, so many creeds, so many paths that wind and wind. When just the art of being kind is all that the sad world needs,' he was to write in his book, *The End of India*. It was a simple answer to all the questions about God and the great doctrines of religion in which, according to Sartre, 'Everything has been worked out except how to live.' He found this simplicity in the words of a mystic singer of Punjab, Bulleh Shah, who sang:

Beshak mandir masjid toro, bulleh shah yeh kehta hai,
Par pyar bhara dil kabhi na toro...jisme dilbar rehta hai.

Khushwant was, however, not one to be satisfied with mysticism alone. Life for him was about the living of it and one of his eternal questions was how should one conduct oneself while living in the world. He went to the Indian ancients, like the Charvakas (600 BC), who encouraged philosophical scepticism and rejected the Vedas. This school of ancient Indian philosophy held only direct perception and experience of reality as sources of knowledge. Khushwant was interested in atheistic and materialistic beliefs, as they had no gods and did not, like other schools of Indian philisophy, say that there should be a turning away or a rejection of life.

Sparring with Dalai Lama

Khushwant found a great interest in the teachings of the Buddha and Jainism, both of which were religions without gods. Though Buddhism was a reformist religion, which had done away with much of the myth, superstition and blind belief of Hinduism, but it still retained the core beliefs of karma and rebirth. It has also, in the centuries since its inception, added its own myths and mystical beliefs. Many changes and different schools of thought had cropped up in Buddhism, as they do in all religions. Though Khushwant studied Buddhism, as he did other religions, he found some of these things unacceptable. The idea of karma and pre-determination also meant the virtual helplessness of men to change their destinies. It also meant, as had happened in India, the acceptance of differences of high and low, and the development of the atrocious caste system, which he detested. Though these evils do not exist in Buddhism, he found that the intricately woven cosmology and fantasy based beliefs in Buddhism, as it had evolved in other countries to which it had spread from India, to be irrational.

The one core belief in Buddhism, that someone like Khushwant perhaps found impossible to accept, was that 'life is suffering.' The entire philosophical basis of Buddhist thought centres around the acceptance, alleviation, and management of such suffering. This went against the most essential belief, of people like Khushwant, in the importance and the supremacy of living a full life. Rejection of life in any form, be it Hindu or Muslim asceticism, or the Buddhist disenchantment with the pain and pleasure of living, went against the grain.

Khushwant asked the Dalai Lama about some of these questions when he met the Tibetan spiritual leader. His announcement, that he was an agnostic, was greeted, as he said, 'with a loud guffaw', from the Dalai Lama. Asked what basis he had to say that God created the world, the monk again floored Khushwant by saying that: 'I do not say God created the world. The Buddha did not say God created the world.' On the contrary, the Dalai Lama said, 'Don't believe in anything that your reason does not accept.' He then asked the Dalai Lama about rebirth and reincarnation, which is one of the basic beliefs of the Buddhists. Again, there was an explosion of laughter from the Dalai Lama, who said Buddhists did believe that people were reborn after death, adding, 'If we did not, I would not be the Dalai Lama.' Khushwant held his ground and was told about instances of children remembering their past lives, but this too has been debunked on many counts. Perhaps the best argument against this is that people who do not believe in rebirth, for instance the Muslims, have no instances of people remembering their past lives.

'No one asks you to believe,' the Dalai Lama said, adding, 'If you can convince me that there is nothing in the theory of reincarnation, I will also reject it.' Once again, the Dalai Lama laughed his deep and carefree laugh. 'If we did not believe in rebirth, I would not be in business,' he said. Karma and rebirth are both the most cleverly devised and seemingly logical beliefs that have ever been created. They seem to answer most questions of destiny, the problem of pain and happiness, and the workings of destiny. They cannot be proved to be true.

Neither can they be proved to be untrue. Neither science nor rationality can ever prove the existence of rebirth and so teachers like the Dalai Lama are on a secure ground when they are asked for providing the proof. Khushwant may not have been convinced but he did say: 'I was exhilarated by being with him. He exuded an aura of goodwill, cheerfulness and crystal clear honesty that envelops you long after you have left his presence.'

Another spiritual teacher in whom Khushwant became interested was UG Krishnamurti, who was regarded highly by his followers in Europe and America. 'UG', as he was widely known, had started out with another spiritual master, Jiddu Krishnamurti, but soon came to have his own following. He had followed the traditional path of Indian seekers, meditated in the Himalaya, sought the counsel of Ramana Maharishi but rejected it, as he did not agree with the Master of Arunachala, who also preached the same ideas about the negation of life.

Khushwant quoted UG in a column: 'I am not a Godman; I would rather be called a fraud...The messy thing, called the mind, has created many destructive things, but the most destructive thing, by far, is God...The variations of God, self-realisation, moksha, liberation etcetera...are pushing man into a state of manic depression.' Khushwant commented also that UG made a mess of his own life. He got married, then deserted his wife and child, and asked for a divorce. He reviewed a book by filmmaker, Mahesh Bhatt, on UG and Khushwant's final comment was that though UG did not want to be God, the book had indeed made him out as one.

It is not a mere coincidence that what attracted Khushwant to some of these spiritual teachers was an essential sense of freedom and informality in their thinking. UG was the ultimate deconstructionist, who believed in nothing and the problem was that, having broken down all accepted ideas of spirituality, he had very little to give to fill up the vacuum. Osho was, of course, another great spiritual deconstructionist and yet, even as he broke down the barriers, he presented the alternatives of a life of freedom and self-realisation through seeing the truth and living with it.

The Guru whom Nehru loved

An extraordinary guru that Khushwant met, in his stubborn propensity to look for unconventional holy people, was a strange and beautiful, or shall we say, once beautiful, woman. He made a great effort to meet one of the most controversial women of Indian spirituality, Shraddha Mata, who had set the newspaper world ablaze when the story came out that she had an affair with Prime Minister Jawaharlal Nehru and it was rumoured that she had his child. Though some reports said it was still born, the stories persisted and sure enough almost 40 years or so after the passing away of Nehru, there were reports of a man in Uttar Pradesh who claimed to be the son of Nehru. Khushwant met Shraddha Mata many times over the years and said that 'Each meeting was for me a memorable one; I became genuinely fond of her.' He had read about Nehru's affair with her in MO Mathai's tell-all book, which said that a child was born to her in a Catholic hospital in South India, but she had abandoned the child and returned to Uttar Pradesh to resume her mission as a tantric sadhavi. Khushwant's first meeting with her was in a dark makeshift hut in the compound of the Nigambodh Ghat cremation ground in Delhi. When he told her his name in that bleak place of burning bodies, she recognised him as the editor of *The Illustrated Weekly of India*. Knowing him to be a journalist, she suddenly exploded and said that he must have come not for her *darshan* but to know more from her about 'what that bastard Mathai had written.' She said it was all a pack of lies.

Khushwant persisted and said that she had met Nehru many times. 'Yes, many times,' she agreed, adding, 'He wrote many letters to me. If he had married again, he would certainly have married me.' 'Then how was it', asked Khushwant, 'that Mrs Gandhi did not know about it.' Her response was that he was being stupid, as such things are not told to daughters. She then asked him if he believed in God and he replied in the negative. Speaking in Hindi, she declared, 'You are full of pride…That is why you write such rubbish.'

A few weeks later, since she had invited him to meet her in Jaipur, Khushwant went there with the photographer Raghu Rai, in a haunted-looking little fortress. 'She must have then been in her 70s…light-skinned and full bosomed. In her younger days, she must have been stunningly beautiful….At some time, when she became a sadhvi, she took to wearing a leopard skin around her middle and started carrying a trishul in her hand. To the anglicised Nehru, she must have looked like an incarnation of the Mother India of his fantasies.'

Khushwant recounted the story of how Nehru had, when he was at the Lucknow circuit house, invited her one evening after his work was done: 'Pandit Ji did what any man would have done to an attractive young woman dressed in no more than a leopard skin. When she wrote to him of its consequences, Pandit Ji stopped writing to her.'

Khushwant mentioned that the lady was very much taken up with the rather good-looking photographer and invited him to spend that night at the Fort where she was staying. 'Raghu funked accepting the invitation', he jested. The next time he visited her, she was having a bath in a tub placed in an open space and she asked him to sit down nearby. 'I could see her from where I sat. She continued talking loudly, as she rubbed herself dry with a towel. It was very titillating.' Once again, she invited Khushwant to spend the night in that fortress. 'I too funked accepting the offer', he conceded.

A 15-year old guru

It seems Khushwant never missed an opportunity to meet the spiritual and religious gurus. Though most of them deserve the harsh criticism and summary dismissal that he gave them in his book on Godmen, Khushwant found some of them worth meeting. One such was Kripalu Maharaj, who although being a self-styled Jagadguru (one of the appellations that Khushwant found unacceptable, like the self-styled Bhagwans, Maharishis and Paramahansas), seemed to have impressed Khushwant. In his own words: 'His scholarship is profound. His memory chapter and verse... He is in short my idea of Jagadguru... I listened to him in spellbound attention.'

A teenager, Balyogeshwar, who was another guru export to the world from India, was on Khushwant's list too. He went to meet him in Mumbai at the Divine Light Mission. The mission, he was told had over four million followers all over the world and Khushwant was intrigued to see the fifteen-year-old boy, who headed this vast organisation. His full title was: 'Yogiraj (king of yogis)Param Sant (first and supreme saint) Satgurudev (true and worshipful teacher) Shri Hansji Maharaj'. The title was as intriguing as his answer to Khushwant's question who wanted to know why people came to him. 'What do they get from you?'

The answer was: 'They come to me because they are unhappy, restless. They want peace. What do they get from me? They get this knowledge that I have.'

Intrepid, as ever, Khushwant persisted, 'Knowledge, what knowledge?'

The answer was simple: 'I tell them of the true aim of

human life. It is not to eat, drink and be merry. It is realisation, the true realisation of God.'

To this, Khushwant answered with his own take on spirituality: 'Surely, it is for everyone to make his own equation with himself and with God. Why must a person have a guru?'

The teenage guru was not disturbed by this. He replied: 'Because without a guru,no one can achieve salvation… Divine knowledge is like money in a bank. It is my money. I have the cheque book. But only after I write on that cheque and sign it, only then can you (as a devotee) draw the money. See?'

Khushwant told him that he was an agnostic, and added,'What is more, I don't think whether there is or there is not, or if a God is very important in human affairs. There are many people like me.'

To this, the young guru asked: 'Then why are you here?'

'Because I am curious', Khushwant replied.

'Curious? Curiosity is a vacuum. You have a vacuum in your mind and want to fill it. That is why you have come to see me', the young guru commented. Khushwant said that curiosity was his profession, as he was a journalist.

At that time, one of the devotees, a foreigner, told Khushwant, 'The guru gave me this knowledge.' Khushwant asked what that knowledge was, but there was no answer. Then Khushwant commented,'I don't understand what the word knowledge means to these people. It sounds like a trinket; you don't have it, then you have it.' Another man from Los

Angeles tipped in to say that he had come to India looking for something, saying, 'Then I met Guru Ji. He gave me this knowledge.' Khushwant's final comment was: "The knowledge continues to elude me."

Tears in his eyes

One guru that Khushwant was impressed with is Mata Amritanandamayi, a spiritual guru of South India, who has a large number of followers. She is known especially for the way in which she greets devotees with a warm hug of spiritual grace.

'In all my life,' Khushwant was to write, 'I have not met a warmer personality than her (the guru). Even an agnostic like me had great difficulty in holding back my tears.'

He had gone to her with his wife and both were engulfed in an embrace. 'She kissed me on both sides of my chest murmuring, 'namo shivaye, namo shivaye'... It was a warm, sensuous hug; I had to hold back my tears. She addressed me as her son, my wife as her daughter. Both of us were a lot older than her parents. This was the thirty-six-year old sadhvi, worshipped by millions of devotees', Khushwant said.

He asked her about death. 'Body is physical and must perish on death,' she said, 'but life continues. It is like an electric bulb, which fuses but the current continues.... Anyhow, why do you ask me questions to which you know the answer?' He said he asked because he did not know and did not believe in life hereafter, because there was no evidence to support it.

Her answer was simple and honest, and perhaps it was the first time that he heard something that was not a doctrine or a blind belief but a realistic explanation. 'You cannot really rule it out,' she said,'in any case, it serves a useful social purpose. You tell a child that if he lies, he will go blind. It is not true but a useful ploy to keep it on the path of truth...There may be some justification to keep the illiterate masses on the right path by threatening them of consequences. But that does not apply to a thinking person. I am quite happy to admit I do not know (the answer to whether there is life after death).'

Her candour and honesty impressed him, and he was learning all the time. Learning but not believing, for it was a special characteristic of an enquiring mind that he would not accept without understanding.

As Khushwant and his wife were leaving, he saw one of the disciples came forward with cubes of ice and these were rubbed on the face and shoulders of Ma Amritanandamayi. He was intrigued and was told that meeting devotees raised her body temperature dangerously and so ice had to be applied to cool her system. His comment was that after having met a sinner like him he was sure she needed extra cubes of ice to get her temperature down.

In his book, *Religion*, Khushwant made a short two-page comment on Swami Vivekananda and ruffled a multitude of feathers in a country where that spiritual leader is still regarded as a driving force of the modern Indian spiritual renaissance. He even took a light pot-shot at the tremendous appreciation and international following that Vivekananda got after his famous Chicago address. He was perhaps quite right in his cynicism when he said that, almost 100 years ago, Vivekananda had said that, because of the disappearance of religiosity in the West, the West would crumble and break down. The truth, of course, was that it was not the West that was breaking down in terms of moral fibre or human values but a highly religious country like India, which was now in the throes of a breakdown of values. This seems true from what we see around us in India today but Khushwant seemed to ignore that the importance of spiritual or moral values has little to do with how men twist their religion and their beliefs to justify their wrong doings. He had either not read enough of Vivekananda, or did not empathise with the idealism and the fiery teachings of the Swami, who had tried to give traditional Hindu thought and philosophy a modern and practical avatar.

At the end of it all, there will always be questions about what he really believed or was looking for. What is certain is that he was the supreme realist who would not, as an intellectual and as a habit of his nature, accept obfuscation and the demand for faith which went against reason. He said that he did not know what people, who spend many hours in prayer and meditation, are looking for. He could understand that disturbed minds in a disturbed world wanted peace of mind.

'However, when it comes to the truth, I am all at sea. But truth with a capital T, they presumably mean reality, the mystery of life, of God. Whether or not they succeed in their search, I do not know… I have yet to meet anyone who claims that he or she has. They only follow others, who they believe have achieved the ultimate,' he said.

His final word on this was that he would like to ask spiritual seekers the question whether it is worth spending so much time and effort to get a vision of the truth 'when the only guarantee of success is God's whim?' He then quoted Dwarka Das Shola's following lines:

Preacher do not abandon the world in the quest of truth.
If you do not find God, you will belong neither here nor there.

Nature was solitude and poetry was priceless

The colours of a writer's canvas

I was talking to an old friend, a professor, who had also known Khushwant. He said something that made me smile,' Do you know that in his second novel, *I Shall Not Hear the Nightingale*, there is no sign of a nightingale?' Having said that, he laughed in his jovial manner. And yet, I have read enough by, and of, Khushwant to know that he was someone who heard the nightingale whenever he wanted and wherever he went. Not just the nightingales, but thrushes, woodpeckers, barbets, blackbirds, and finches that he looked for and found in the midst of whatever it was that he was doing. He also looked for the flowering vines, the *madhumalati, the jabbakusum,raat ki rani* and dozens of other flowers, bushes and trees whose names he knew or sometimes did not. He found them on the road sides of the lush Lutyen's Delhi where he moved about.

An affair with nature

With all his fame and books, and commitments to a life in writing, Khushwant found the time and the awareness to look at nature all around him, to make notes and record observations in his nature diary. He had always loved walking and often spoke about his long walks, which went on for many hours, up in the hills of Shimla. Living in his early days at his father's villa in Mashobra, some 30 miles to the north of Shimla, he often set himself free, as he took the winding hill roads and mountain paths, cutting through dense forests and waiting silences. Somehow and wherever he was, he found the lonely woods, the great trees that were sanctuaries for a roaming and a restless mind. He found the birds that poured their song on him in days of sunshine and he found the lakes where he would shed his clothes and his concerns, and swim in blissful abandon.

'More than anything else,' he has written, 'I love going for long walks. When walking out beyond Shimla, I explored other mountain roads. There were solitary shaded paths that ran through a pine and fir forest to an Italian monastery. Another went steeply uphill from Mashobra to a small orchard, called Dane's Folly, towards Wild Flower Hall... During the rainy season, the valley was often covered by mists. Mysteriously, the mists would lift and the sun would break out to light the rain-washed emerald green hillsides and set the stream,which ran between them, sparkling in the light.'

Later, when he settled in Delhi, he lived in a green island in the city; his house surrounded by four verdant plant nurseries, a square park of old trees and bushes in the centre of a complex of houses, and a small but bountiful patch of green at the back of his house. Here he spent many an afternoon in the winter, watching the birds, as they shied away from his over-a-dozen cats (his granddaughter's pets) and writing notes in his diary. Though in his later years, he could not move too far out in the green environs of the city that he loved, Khushwant kept that diary with him or just made notes in his mind wherever he was, as he went about his daily life. The diary became a smorgasbord of the way he saw nature all around him. It was brought together in his book, *Nature Watch*, which is sometimes rapturous and sometimes contains a gentle conversation that he was having with his readers about trees and fruits, flowers and birds, and even snakes and insects. It was patterned after traditional songs, *Baramaasi* (song of the twelve months of a year) of Indian poets.

Along with the descriptions and stories of nature,in that book, there are also poems on natural phenomenon by various great poets, such as Kalidasa, Bharatihari, Guru

Nanak, Meer, Ghalib, Akbar Ilahabadi, Tagore and many others. It was a spectacular performance in which Khushwant brought together the two great loves of his life, nature and poetry.

He had studied the works of various English poets in a big way while studying in England and had even met some great contemporary poets like Dylan and Auden. Among his favourites, in the classical English tradition, were Tennyson, Shakespeare, Browning and Wordsworth. Later however, when he was in Lahore, he was introduced by his friend, Manzur Qadir, to the treasure of Urdu poetry. The classical Urdu poets like Zauq, Meer, Momin, Ghalib and Zafar then stayed with him all his life, along with the modern Urdu poets like Allama Iqbal, Jaan Nissar Akhtar and the contemporary Javed Akhtar.

And even nature was sexy

Nature Watch, became a book that has never gone off the bookshelves. It is, of course, a record of his observations of nature and does what nature writing is supposed to do - to take the reader into the sanctuary of the green world around him. But something in this book that makes it so well loved is the presence of Khushwant himself at all times. His stories tell of the sometimes playful and sometimes cruel caprices of nature's beings, and there is always the humour and the amused, but childlike, wonder of the writer. And since the 'incorrigible Sardar' could not be but himself, there are also vastly amusing descriptions of 'shameless' birds mating.

Much of his nature watching was done during his early morning trips to Delhi's Gymkhana Club, where he went for his customary swim or a game of tennis. There, on the great older trees in the club environs, he followed the antics of the birds when his eye was not on the tennis ball. He said: 'Big birds are much in evidence on big trees. One morning in the Gymkhana Club, I saw a pair of hornbills fly to a semul tree where a couple of pariah kites were mating, screaming in ecstasy and agony. They watched the goings-on with great interest. Lapwings were also scandalized by the kites' shameless behaviour. They flew around the tree loudly enquiring 'Did ye do it? Did ye do it?' I wanted to shout back, 'I did not, but take a look at those kites!"

His interest in nature was something that he quite consciously cultivated and worked upon, as with almost everything else that he did. He recounted that he felt he had to know the names and other information about trees, shrubs and flowers. To do so, he acquired books by nature writers, among them the great Indian ornithologists, Saleem Ali, and environmentalist, Zafar Futehally. He also tried to talk and meet with birdwatchers and horticulturists, and as his nature knowledge increased. He even ventured to go out and give talks on Delhi's natural phenomena on All India Radio (AIR) and the national television, Doordarshan. As a journalist and a writer, this hankering after information was part of his magic formula of holding the interest of his reader. He often said to debutant writers and journalists that if the reader does not find something interesting to read, he will not read you.

Much of his nature watching was done in the private back garden of his house in Delhi where he had a small rectangular plot of green, bordered with sprays of many coloured Bougainville. In his book, *Nature Watch*, the following simple description, without any frills, seems to make you sit by his side in the sunshine of his garden: 'There is a small patch of grass with some lime, orange, and grapefruit trees, and a pomegranate tree. I do not grow many flowers, a bush of Gardenia, a couple of jasmine and a, queen of the night (raat ki rani)…I have placed a bird bath, which is shared by sparrows, crows, mynahs, kites, pigeons, babblers and a dozen stray cats, which have made my home theirs…what perhaps accounts for the profusion of birdlife…are the several nurseries in the vicinity, the foliage of many trees and bushes cannabis sativa (bhang)… Also, there are lots of butterflies, beetles, wasps and bees, and bugs of different kinds.'

To find something that endures

Khushwant, the nature writer, journeyed through the months of the year, recording the changes in seasons, the going of the harsh summer sunshine, as the rains come down on the city and the sprawling, his beloved, Lodhi Gardens, and then the mists and the cold bite of winter. It is the journey of a lover of poetry, a lover of all beauty, a writer who turns from the complexities of life and human circumstances to the simplicity and the blissful regularity of nature, and finds therein something that endures. The greatest poets and writers of the world, in every culture and every language have done this they have turned to nature when everything else begins to burden the soul. The book, *Nature Watch*, is essentially Khushwant's song of the seasons in the best tradition of the great classical Sanskrit poet, Bharatrihari, who describes the passage of days and years in ecstatic poetry:

The cycle recurrence of sunset and dawn
daily serves to measure life's decay;
but burdened in his mundane tasks,
man does not grasp time's fugitive flight.
Seeing old age, pain and death,
he is not aroused to anxiety;
drunk on delicious heady wine,
the world is made in a oblivion.

Amidst all the beauty of nature, he also saw the cruelty that is part of the canvas of life. Even in a nature diary, which celebrates the colours, the songs, and the seasons of the year, Khushwant, the raconteur, has a story: 'for years, a redstart (perhaps more than one) had been spending its winter months in my little patch of garden. It was a friendly little bird, twitching its tail after every hop, as it moved closer to my chair on the lawn, also somewhat foolish in equating me with my cats. One evening, I saw a few scarlet feathers on the lawn and realised that my cats have brought the redstart to bid me farewell forever.'

The 'Grand Saint' in Italy

Since he travelled extensively in his earlier years, Khushwant had an opportunity to extend his love of nature to other countries. The people, the places and the cultures were all different and he enjoyed them all, but most of all, he enjoyed the one thing that was a familiar and unchanging - the voices and the hues of nature. This is a story about Khushwant's month-long stay in Italy, in 1970, when he had been invited by the Rockefeller foundation to spend a month at Grand Hotel Villa Serbelloni, situated on a hill overlooking Lake Como, in northern Italy. Since he used to play tennis every day at that time, he missed the tennis court at the villa he decided to make up with a swim in the lake instead. Either there was no swimsuit available, or he decided to simply carry on with his mandatory Sikh *kachcha* (underwear shorts), he made quite a sight as he walked down the hill and splashed his way across the lake with carefree abandon. Since he was all alone, he had time to enjoy the natural beauty all around him. The icing on the cake was that, in those Elysium surroundings, the nightingales were singing. As he was to clarify once, it is a false notion that nightingales sing only at night, for, as he had observed, the birds break into song at any time of the day or night.

After the swim, he would emerge like a dishevelled mermaid, with his abundant hair opened out and hanging to his waist to dry out in the Italian sunshine, the water droplets streaming down his body. He would then climb the hill on the other side, get back into the water and swim mightily across back to the villa. It was a daily ritual for Khushwant, who was then about fifty years old and in the pink of his physical condition. The ritual was followed, with great fascination, by the locals living near the lake, who were mostly peasants, cultivating the fields and raving sheep around the slopes near Lake Como. Nothing they had heard of, or seen before, had prepared them for the sight of a well-built Sikh, with a profusion of hair snaking down his shoulders with nothing on but the *kachcha*, and that too in the middle of an Italian lakefront villa, which once belonged to a lord. The story goes that, as a couple of weeks passed, and still the Sardar with flowing hair came every morning, the locals had convinced themselves that the vision they saw in the bright sunlight every morning was that of a saint, II Santo. By the end of his stay, Khushwant had been fully ordained a saint to the rank of 'great saint', or II Santo Grande.

Many years after Khushwant's return from Italy, this story continued to be told in that little village. One of the peasants would say: 'Do you not remember the murder of the old woman at the inn?...It happened the summer following the visit of II Santo Grande.'

The sadness of the sparrows

Perhaps one of the most beautiful passages of writing from Khushwant came both from his love for deep relationships and his love for nature. It is an unforgettable piece of writing almost at the very end of his story, The Portrait of a Lady. In this beautiful story, about his relationship with his grandmother from his childhood to his youth, Khushwant created the magic of her love that was selfless and gave him a sense of belonging and safety in his childhood. It was his grandmother who first taught him the Sikh scriptures and the verses of the Gurus when he was a child and catered to his every whim. When he grew up, he was given a room of his own and his grandmother was left on her own. She accepted the seclusion with resignation and kept herself busy with her spinning wheel, which she worked on from sunrise to sunset, as she recited her prayers. In the afternoon, she would relax and sit on the veranda, breaking bread into little bits for the little birds that gathered around her, 'creating a veritable bedlam of chirruping...Some came and perched on her legs others on her shoulders. Some even sat on her head. She smiled but never shooed them away. It used to be the happiest half hour of the day for her.'

As the story moves, he went abroad for further studies. Before he left, he thought his grandmother would be upset. However, she was not even sentimental; she came to see him off at the railway station. She did not talk or show any emotion, as her lips moved in a prayer. She kissed him goodbye. When he returned after some years and, as she hugged him, he could hear her reciting her prayers. Even on that day of his arrival, her happiest moments were with her sparrows whom she fed for a longer time. The next day, she sang songs with the women of the village about the homecoming of the warriors. But, for the first time on that day, she did not pray. She was taken ill the next morning with a mild fever, which did not subside and during the day, she laid peacefully, with her lips moving in a prayer. Nobody even noticed when her lips stopped moving.

As the men lifted her and laid her on the ground, they went to make arrangements for her cremation. When they came back, 'The sun was setting and had lit up her room and the veranda with a blaze of golden light…all over the veranda and in her room right up to it. She lay dead and still wrapped in the red shroud, thousands of sparrows sat scattered on the floor but there was no chirruping. We felt sorry for the birds and my mother fetched some bread. She broke it into little crumbs the way my grandmother used to and threw it to them. The sparrows took no notice of the bread. When we carried my grandmother's corpse away, they flew away quietly. Next morning, the sweeper swept the breadcrumbs into the dustbin.'

The poetry of such a passage was something that lay deep within Khushwant. And even he could not always, as is true of all creative artists, summon up the muse whenever he wanted. He wrote all his life and every day, for he was a professional writer but even he must have known that the great flights of inspiration come but once in a while. Also apart from the business of writing, about life and its emotional complexities, there was much else that he had to say, which he said in his journalism, his columns, his lectures and in the evenings of jest and banter, which he held forth upon the world and its people. And yet, even as he laughed and spoke and cracked his jokes, one could sometimes see that his mind was somewhere else, that he was always observing, thinking and moving beyond the moment to try to understand the laughter and the sadness and the beauty. 'A life well lived is the only religion,' he had often said and a life well lived meant an entire world of experience.

Poetry and the spirit of Ghalib

Poetry gave him the richness of thought and the mystical freedom that is perhaps sought by every creative artiste. He kept a collection of the poems written by Mirza

Ghalib by his bedside and often called that great mystical poet of Delhi his 'companion', especially in the days when he lived alone at his home after his wife's death. It became a bond stretching across time between the two men of free intellect and deep individualism. He was to say once that he seemed to have developed a split personality in the sense that a great diversity of thought and feeling seemed to coalesce in him almost seamlessly.

'I have come to the conclusion that I have been an impostor all my life. I have written several books on the religion and the history of the Sikhs...without having ever read the Guru Granth Sahib from cover to cover. Nevertheless, when people refer to me as a scholar of Sikhism, I protest so mightily that they think I am being modest.' He goes on to say, in explaining the diversity (or contradictions, for want of a better word) in his life, that he read the Sikh Scriptures in the morning: 'I devote my afternoons to reading all the poets from Meer to Ghalib to Faiz...The mornings are devoted to reading about praise of the Lord... spiritual elevation, the need to conquer lust and anger; and then in the evenings, it is poetry about women and boys with rosy cheeks and rounded bottoms...in short, it is the temple in the a.m. the tavern after p.m. I have become a split personality.'

And then, he thinks of the poet that he so loves: 'I comfort myself by believing that Mirza Ghalib must have faced the same dilemma.' And indeed, Ghalib never did say his prayers regularly, broke many Islamic taboos, especially with his love for alcohol. Khushwant seemed to revel in the similarity between himself and Ghalib. Both had a love-hate relationship with God (even though Khushwant denied any relationship, much of his life was spent thinking and writing about God), both laughed at the pomposity and the sham piousness of people, and both cared nothing for what the world had to say about what they did or what they said.

It was, for Khushwant, a friendship with a man who had lived a couple of centuries ago, a friendship of his deep loneliness. It was not just his loneliness after his wife's passing away, but a loneliness that perhaps stayed with him all his life, in spite of the laughter and the noise and frenzy of living. Talking about his evening drink of Scotch, which had become perhaps the most famous and well-known evening ritual in the country, Khushwant even felt that, much like him, Ghalib too sat down in the evenings and opened his bottle of Scotch and watched the sun go down.

'By the time the day is over and that time is close for my sundowner, I am a thoroughly confused person,' Khushwant wrote and added,'I pour myself a peg of Scotch 'n' soda...I come to the comforting conclusion: 'impostor' is too strong a word for me, but 'humbug" fits me to a tee.'

As always, he could laugh at himself. A life of struggle to realise himself and to find the blossoming of his talent, a life spent in closely witnessing the lives and the events that go on relentlessly and his own ways of thinking that moved from perceived experience to the wisdom of acceptance and understanding. All this had, at some level, made him conscious of the absurdity, in a philosophical sense, of life. There seem to be no inherent value and meaning in life, and most people were lost in the inability to find that meaning. Perhaps, in the metaphysical rebellion of Ghalib, he found the same futility of being unduly serious and of being able to laugh at the sacred, as well as the profane.

He found the same quality in other poets too, for the poet tries in his flights of imagination to see some truth and beauty in all the weakness and the dross that fills the lives of people. Khushwant's love for poetry continued all his life and through all the years of journalism, and the writing of new novels, his many books, not to forget the series of joke books, he continued not only to read mainly Urdu poetry, but also to venture into difficult and painstaking translations to make that poetry available to English readers. 'The poet', writes Anais Nin, 'is one who is able to keep the fresh vision of the child alive.' When the writings and the columns and the socialising were done, Khushwant turned to poetry, for as he said, 'poetry is priceless.'

In his younger days, he could recite English poetry by rote for hours, for such was his memory. Later, Urdu poetry took over and he memorised the greats like Ghalib, Iqbal,

Faiz, Hafeez and Ahmed Faraz amongst others. As was his wont, he made an effort. He wrote about the English poets whom he loved but who seemed to fade from memory and, therefore, he kept many anthologies of English poetry near him. He also had the King James Bible, the Guru Granth Sahib and various books of Urdu poetry, most loved of them all being Ghalib at his bedside. 'There is great wisdom in the poetry I love and read. I recite my favourite lines whenever I get a chance…There are poems for every mood and emotion', he said.

There was romance and mysticism, rebellion and carelessness about life in Ghalib and the other great Urdu poets like Momin and Zauq and Faiz that seemed to strike a chord. Among his favourite verses, he quoted the poet Ibrahim Zauq:

Laayi hayat, aayee qazaa, le chali chale
Apni khushi na aaye the na apni khushi chale
....Behtar to tha yehi ki duniya se na dil lage
Par kya karein jo kaam na be-dillagi chale
(Life brought me here and when the end came I went away,
Neither did I come by my own, will nor I go with my will
… It would have been better not to fall in love with the world, but what can one do if it is impossible to live without such love.)

For Khushwant, however, Ghalib was the greatest Urdu poet ever. The poet was born in Agra in1797 and then lived most of his life in Delhi. His house in the walled city area of Ballimaran is still to be seen as a monument to this great poet of Delhi. His father was a soldier but Ghalib decided to live by the pen.

Khushwant notes, perhaps with some fellow feeling, that 'Ghalib was a non-conformist and a bon viveur. Though he revered Allah and the Prophet, he never said his five daily prayers, never fasted during Ramadan, and never went on pilgrimage to Mecca. He preferred French wines but also liked Scotch, which he imbibed every evening while he composed poetry.' And one can almost feel the glee when Khushwant tells about the time when a friend told Ghalib that the prayers of a person who drank wine were never granted. On hearing this, he said: 'My friend, if a man has wine, what else he needs to pray for?'

One of his favourite verses from Ghalib has been quoted by Khushwant in his books as well as in his columns:

Ishq se tabiyat ne zeest ka mazaa payaa,
Dard ki davaa payee, dard-e-la-davaa paya

(*Love gave me the lust for living, to ease my pain it gave me something for sure; it gave me such pain that nothing can cure.*)

And as the impecunious poet Ghalib wandered nearly 200 years ago in the narrow lanes of old Delhi, heavily in debt and sometimes lauded for his poetry, but often times scorned for his almost heretical sense of humour, his carelessness with the pious and the nobility, Khushwant probably walked with him in his mind's eye, following the thoughts and marvelling at the way the two men in different ages could see the truth with such clarity. Khushwant was a passionate 'Delhi-wallah', who enjoyed the composite culture, the love for Urdu, the poetry and the stories of romance and eccentricity that abounded in this historic city. He wrote a book with photographer. Raghu Rai, on the city, which has existed from the times of the Pandavas and seen the rule of Muslim conquerors, the Mughals and the British. The book *Delhi: A Portrait*, took the writer and the photographer to the old and the new parts of the city but much of the true romance was felt by both in old Delhi, which has an enduring character of its own. And as he took his notes, walking along the lanes spreading out from the central point of Jama Masjid to the ancient localities, he must have enjoyed the feeling of having walked in the poet's footsteps. He quoted:

Naqsh faryadi hai kis kee shoukhiye tehreer ka
Kaghaz hi pairahan hai paikar-e-tasveer ka

(*A picture speaks for itself, what learning and exposition does it need? The paper on which it is painted is only its outer garment; it tells its own tale indeed.*)

And then perhaps, as age came upon him, Khushwant grew closer to Ghalib with verses such as these:

Go haath mein jumbish nahin, aankhon mein to dum hai
Rehne do abhee sagar-o-meena mere aage

(Though I can no longer stretch my hands, I still have the strength in my eyes. Let the jug of wine and the cup remain before me.)

A fascination for Iqbal

It is interesting to recall that, in some ways, his writing life started when he was a diplomat in London but got tired of a repetitive and meaningless life. He had then turned, on a whim that seemed to nudge him towards destiny, to translating the Sikh scripture, the *Japji Sahib*. In the later years, he would do many more translations of scriptural texts and hymns of the Sikh Gurus and would also, following the diverse reaches of his mind, go on to work at translations of such classical works as Allama Iqbal's *Shikwa* and *Jawab-e-Shikwa*.

Muhammad Iqbal (1877-1938) had his ancestral home in Kashmir in an ancient family of Brahmins.He was a second generation Muslim, as his father, Rattan Lal, had converted to Islam and was disowned by his Kashmiri Pandit family, Saprus. Iqbal himself became one of the greatest poets of his time and was often compared to none other than Ghalib. His mother tongue was Punjabi but he never wrote in it and used only Pushto and Urdu. He was knighted in 1922 and became Sir Muhammad Iqbal. He is famous in India for having written the patriotic song, *Sare jahan se achcha*, but his real destiny lay in the promotion of the formation of Pakistan. He was strongly influenced by Jinnah and the Muslim league. In fact, he became a passionate activist for the formation of Pakistan and was among the front line of Muslim leaders in the late 1930s to raise the demand for the partition of India.

Khushwant was deeply impressed by the poetry of Iqbal and chose to translate his epic poems, *Shikwa* and *Jawab-e-Shikwa* into English. The poems are a dialogue with Allah and though they are a great example of Islamic poetry, they are also universal in their symbolism as a supplication by man who complains to his God and then gets a reply. Khushwant worked hard at the translation but, as in all such ventures, was met with praise as well as criticism. The *Shikwa* poems had become part of the religious culture of Pakistan and had been used in plays, *qawallis* and popular performances. The poems bemoan the plight of Muslims all over the world and complain to Allah of having let them down. It is not a bit surprising that Khushwant, a man of no religion or God, should have chosen to work on this deeply religious work of poetry. He has said that Iqbal was a great poet but had become fanatical in his view of Islam. In spite of that, however, Khushwant valued the work of Iqbal purely on its literary merit. Iqbal's obsession with his religion, and his strong activism for the Muslim cause, was quite another thing. The poet is regarded as one of the founding fathers of Pakistan and his tomb, which is close to the Badshahi mosque in Lahore, is a national monument.

In spite of his political predilections, the poetry of Iqbal rises far above his obsession with his religion. A fine example of this is the fact that his unforgettable poem for India, *Saare jahan se achcha*..., has never been rivalled as an Indian patriotic song. It was a strange quality of his muse that his passion for Pakistan in his poetry transcended to a sensitive portrayal of the human condition. One of his major themes was the idea of '*khudi*,' or selfhood, being strong willed to realise one's goals, being brave in self-confidence. One of his often quoted verses is about this:

Khudi ko kar buland itna
Ki har taqdeer se pehley
Khuda bandey se yeh poochey
Bataa teri raza kya hai...
(*Steel your will with such power*
that at every turn of fate it be so
that God should ask of men,
'Tell me, what is it that you wish to do?')

This team of the inherent quality of man, being a heroic and an undefeated presence in the universe, is repeated in another famous verse which Khushwant put into English:

Tu shaheen hai parwaz hai kaam hai
Tere samne aasman aur bhi hain...
(*You are a falcon, it is in your nature to fly*
for you there are others skies beyond this guy

don't let the web of dons and dusks enmesh you
for you have other lives, other goals to pursue
beyond these stars are worlds yet to unearth
there are more trials of love to test your worth.)

However Iqbal's great popularity bordering on veneration in Pakistan, where he has been given the highest honours and titles of that nation, is built as much on his universalism and flights of poetry as much as on his concern for the well-being of Islam and Muslims everywhere. In the following verses, Iqbal gives an example of his love for Islam:

Akl hai tere sipar, ishq hai teri shamsheer…

(*With reason as your shield and the sword of love in your hand,*
servant of God, the leadership of the world is at your command!
The cry, 'Allah-o-Akbar' destroys all except God; it is a fire.
If you are true Muslims, your destiny is to grasp what you aspire.
What is this miserable world? To write the world's
History, pen and table are offered to you.)

A romantic monk's poetry

Though Urdu poetry was avowedly a passion with him, Khushwant enjoyed poetry anywhere he found it. On a visit to see the Dalai Lama, he asked for some Tibetan poetry and, as luck would have it, he was given a book of poems written by the Sixth Dalai Lama, who was enthroned in 1697. As it turned out the Sixth Dalai Lama, Tsanyang Gyatso, was an enigma, and a poet. He loved the great outdoors, archery and refused to be disciplined or to be bound down by vows of celibacy. 'For him,'wrote Khushwant, 'it was the monastery and prayer by daytime, taverns, drinks, songs of love and pretty Tibetan maidens at night.' Most certainly,he was a man after his own heart. The book of poems, *Songs of the Sixth Dalai Lama*, had some remarkable poems, more so for having been written by a spiritual leader.

Even if meditated upon,
The face of my Lama comes not to me
But again and again comes to me
The smiling face of my beloved.

As Khushwant read these poems, he came to the conclusion that this irrepressible holy man seemed to have admitted defeat in the pursuit of the spiritual:

If I could meditate upon the dhamma
As intensely as I must on my beloved
I would certainly attain enlightenment
Surely, in this one lifetime.
In another poem he writes:
'If the maiden will live for ever
The wine will flow ever more
The tavern is my refuge
With wine, I am content.

This strange spiritual leader,the Sixth Dalai Lama, of the Tibetans ultimately fell out with the Regent and his reign came to an end in 1706. He had been the supreme spiritual leader of the Tibetan Buddhists for nine years. Khushwant's comment after reading his poetry is cryptic: 'It is incredible that in a highly conservative and religion-oriented society like the Tibetans, it is the iconoclastic Sixth Dalai Lama who remains the great favourite.'

A Sikh and an agnostic

He kept an enriching balance

Khushwant was often asked about his visits to gurudwaras because he was loud in saying that he believed neither in religion, nor in God. Yet, one of his first literary works was an English translation of the *Japji Sahib* verses from the Sikh Scriptures. He retained his turban and Sikh identity all his life, lived the Punjabi and Sikh culture, and spoke the Punjabi language. His answer to the question about visits to gurudwaras was a simple admission. 'A contradiction,' he would say, 'and leave it at that'.

As in most things about him, he let people draw their own conclusions. As long as he did what he thought was right, behaved in a manner that satisfied his well thought out positions, other things did not matter. In fact, contradictions do exist because rigid assumptions persist in our minds and that assumed the ideas or systems are incontrovertible and come with a set of rules that have necessarily to be followed. So it is that every belief system becomes doctrine and all other doctrine is to be rejected. Truth, which is what religions seek, is divided into separate compartments. He did admit that some contradictionsmay have appeared his way of life and thinking. But they were contradictions only for others.

Khushwant could not be limited by doctrine, for freedom of thought was his very nature. He chose what he wanted to believe in. In an interview once about his religion, he went on to quote his old friend, Nirad C Chaudhri, who he often said was in his discussions on religion, especially Hinduism. In his books, such as *The Continent of Circe,* Nirad had once said that, of all the religions in the world, which put people in straight jackets, Hinduism was the freest and perhaps the cleverest. He had said that a Hindu was a Hindu by birth and as he grew, to childhood and youth and even later, he did not have to, by any rule of the religion, observe any rituals or austerities. He remained a Hindu whatever he did, as long as he did not convert to any other religion. There were no rules and regulations to be followed. Even if he never went to a temple or ever offered prayer of any kind, if he decided to get back to his religion of birth even just before his death, he would be a Hindu for all practical purposes. Khushwant liked to quote this to emphasise that you can be part of a religion, especially the religion of your birth, without following every ritual, rule and belief.

His fondness for Sikhism was also because of the fact that he had been born in a very devout family of Sikhs, in a close-knit Sikh community in a small village in what is now Pakistan. The community stayed together and all festivals, family events and also the times of tension were experienced together. Khushwant was introduced to the Sikh Scriptures at an early age of five years by his very devout grandmother. This followed the pattern of what used to happen at that time in the families of all communities where the elders introduced children to the richness of their religious heritage. Right up to his teenage years, he lived in the awareness of his community and the Sikh culture. It was something he never forgot. Though his thinking and beliefs changed, as he left his village for education in Delhi and then in London, Sikhism had become part of his very being. He became a free thinker soon after his London days, and his vast reading and deep deliberation about religion and God, based on his experiences and worldview, combined to create a very individual understanding of religious matters. What is important to note is that he remained a very committed Sikh all his life and was deeply concerned about what happened to people of his community. He saw nothing sectarian about this. He felt a strong empathy for all who were exploited.

Khushwant's war on Khalistan

It was way back in 1971 that strident demands for a separate theocratic state for the Sikhs were made by Jagjit Singh Chouhan, who travelled extensively in the USA, Canada and the UK to garner support for his demand. Khalistan soon became a major issue at the time as millions of dollars were collected in funds and a flag was raised, and the republic of Khalistan was announced from US soil. Khushwant opposed this strongly and from the very beginning. However, it was not something that would go away and strong reverberations of the Khalistan movement were felt in Punjab, fuelled also by support from Pakistan. An ally to the cause was found in the shape of a fiery Sikh preacher from the interior of Punjab, Jarnail Singh Bhindranwale, who was to hold centre stage in the violence and aggression that ripped across Punjab for almost two decades.

Khushwant wrote extensively against this and obviously it did not make him popular with a large section of Sikhs who supported Khalistan and Bhindranwale. Khushwant's hatred against those who are demanding Khalistan was well known. 'Khalistan over my dead body,' he said once during the course of an interview.

'Bhindranwale had threatened me that I would be liquidated if I wrote against him. Two other journalists who accompanied me were very petrified. I wrote the piece under able guidance of Manohar Shyam Joshi Ji, who was then editing Weekend Review and did not take a by-line on the piece,' Khushwant said.

When reminded of this incident of Bhindranwale threatening him, which took place in June 1982, Khushwant dismissed him in two words; 'A rat,' he said. Talking of his meeting with Bhindranwale, Khushwant recalled: 'A year later when I met Bhindernwale in the Golden Temple complex, he asked me how come I was still alive. "I told him, I am alive because Wahe Guru is with me.'"When Bhindranwale died during Operation Blue Star, Khushwant conceded that he died like a man.

Khushwant, at one stage, decided that he wanted to find out about Bhindranwale's growing fame in Punjab. He made a special visit to the Golden Temple complex to find out the truth.

He spoke to every conceivable person who could shed light on the growing popularity of the man who would carry an iron arrow while doing parkirma on the Darbar Sahib Complex to impress his followers.

'At the Darbar Sahib complex, during 1982 and 1983, four to five hundred persons were administered. Amrit each Wednesday and Sunday. On 13 April 1983, over ten thousand people were initiated and during the month ending on 13 April 1984, forty-five thousand Sikhs received Amrit. This revival was extremely significant and Sant Bhindranwale was emerging as the leading figure in the Sikh faith and a role-model for the youth. I was once told by a relative that his two sons had stopped taking tea. I asked him why, and if they had been to (the Golden Temple complex) to see Sant Bhindranwale. The reply was: 'No, it is just the way things are in Punjab. The young people love and admire him so much that if they come to know what the Sant does or doesn't do, they like to follow his example.' People sought his advice and intercession for personal problems and conflict resolution.'

The tricks of popularity

Khushwant reported: 'On a later visit to Amritsar, I got tinkling into the reasons of Bhindranwale's popularity. I will narrate two incidents to illustrate this. One day, a young girl came to see Bhindranwale…She clutched his feet and sobbed out her story of how she was maltreated by her husband's family for failing to extract more money from her parents and of her husband's unwillingness to take her side. Bhindranwale asked her name and where she lived.

'So, you are a daughter of the Hindus,' he said. 'Are you willing to become the daughter of a Sikh?' She nodded. Bhindranwale sent a couple of his armed guards to fetch the girl's family. An hour later, a very frightened trio consisting of the girl's husband and his parents were brought to his presence. 'Is this girl a daughter of your household?' he demanded. They admitted she was. 'She tells me that you want money from her father. I am her father.' He placed a tray full of currency notes before them and told them: "Take whatever you want" The three fell at his feet and craved forgiveness.'

But little did the people who witnessed this realize that the same woman and her in-laws were part of a drama that Bhindranwale would enact whenever he was in a mood to impress. A senior ranking police officer of Punjab police revealed this after the incident.

Khushwant's outspoken opposition to Bhindranwale made him a target and, as a result, he received death threats from the supporters of Khalistan. He received a high level security cover at his house from the government which he hated, but went along with it. He was asked about this Don't ask me. The officers of Delhi police told me that my house was surveyed by terrorist, Harjinder Singh Jinda, and they have recovered a map of the house. So they have given me the security cover. But I am sick and tired of them already.

Right through the day, I have to give them tea four times in a day, two meals and allow them to use the loo as well. I have to spend more on them in a month in comparison to the cheques I get for my writing. I have told the Delhi police chief that I do not want security cover any more. One of the security inspectors wants everything to be cooked in pure ghee. They will leave shortly,' he said.

A sectarian movement

Though Bhindranwale was considered a Sant (saint) and a great leader of the Sikhs, Khushwant saw through that and felt it was just another sectarian movement, based on the intolerance and fundamentalist mentality, that he had always opposed. He saw in Bhindranwale a clever mixture of an almost quixotic zeal to re-establish a revanchist idea of Sikhism on the one hand; and, on the other hand, were his cunning and street smart quiver of tactics to find popularity and blind devotion among the rustic people of the Punjab.

Once on a visit to Delhi, Bhindranwale insisted on getting into a train compartment with his horse. Though it was a matter of no significance, the media picked it up everywhere and, for the common people and the Sikhs, it was an example of his being a committed warrior who would not travel without his horse. On another occasion, Khushwant commented on seeing Bhindranwale speak at a rally that many of the actions of the man, even his dress and mannerisms, were meant to remind people of the actions of the Gurus. He particularly mentioned, in this context, Bhindranwale's way of holding an arrow in his hand as he spoke. Centuries ago, it was Guru Gobind Singh, who held an arrow in his hand at most occasions.

Khushwant also, in his opposition to Khalistan, had a running fight with Jagjit Singh Chouhan, who had raised the so-called flag of Khalistan.

He once wrote that Chouhan had been a shorn Sikh in his native village in Punjab. This was highly damaging, as now that man was fighting for the purest and most traditional form of Sikhism. Chouhan instituted a defamation case against Khushwant in a London court. But the court took a dim view of the case. Chouhan, in a sense, won the case but it was a putative victory. He was given a redressal of exactly one penny in the form of penalty. Khushwant was asked to meet the expenses for the case.

His pen was his sword

Khushwant was obviously not concerned with power politics and became the voice of sanity for most people, Sikhs as well as non-Sikhs, who wanted to live in peace in a secular India. His columns were published in many languages and, more than English, the columns in Gurmukhi had a wide ranging impact among different sections of the Sikhs. He used his pen with bravery, like a sword, in an atmosphere of threats and violence. It was a turbulent time of politics in Punjab and though Khushwant met leaders of various sects and political parties, he stuck to his anti-fundamentalist views. This made him accepted and popular among right-thinking people everywhere, especially among the Punjabis and, particularly, the Sikhs.

Amanpreet Singh Gill, an academician and writer, observes that Punjabi writers and intellectuals were fully supportive of Khushwant, so he was not alone in his fight against Sikh fundamentalism. He writes: 'Khushwant Singh came to my world through *Gurmukhi*. He was writing a lot on the Punjab crisis after 1984 and his column was published in Gurmukhi newspapers as well. Balwant Gargi had included his pen sketch in his book *Hasin Chehre* (Beautiful Faces). Ajit Caur (a prolific and well known Punjabi writer, and featured in chapter 12 of this book) followed with her collection of pen sketches published by *Navyug*. Gulzar Singh Sandhu never missed an opportunity to mention his proximity with Khushwant. For the Punjabi world of letters, he was larger than life.

'When Khushwant Singh completed his work, *A History of Sikhs*, he wrote two Latin words at the end: *opus exegi* (now the work is done). Khushwant had spent his childhood in a non-Sikh region of Punjab. The Sikh presence in this region was a product of the Sikh rule but it had ended seventy years ago. His native village, Hadali, was known for record breaking recruitment of Muslims in the British army during the first World War. His father was busy building a new capital for the (British) empire in Delhi and his village was proud to send its young men to serve as cannon fodder to Europe. Empire was seen as the benefactor of Punjab and of the Sikhs also. He was a fourth generation Kesadhari Sikh and he was aware that army recruitment and growth of Kesadhari Sikh was a parallel development.' (In his early days in London, he had also written, perhaps a bit impetuously, that if Sikh identity was not maintained by the young, very soon there would be no difference between Hindus and Sikhs).'

This was the reason for his interest in writing *A History of the Sikhs*. It has remained the popular reading from the day it was written in the 60s to this time. The major strength of this work was its use of sources. Khushwant used mainly English, Persian and Gurmukhi works as his sources. Among the English works, there were colonial works and works of introductory scholarship. There were also memoirs, commentaries, journals and travelogues. Among the Persian works, he used unpublished manuscripts and a few published ones. Some of his sources are never consulted again in works of the Sikh history.

Sikhism was a bridge

Khushwant explained the rise of Sikhism in the context of rise of Punjabi nationalism. He saw Sikhism as a bridge between the Hindu and Muslim world views. His views on the Sikh kingdom of Ranjit Singh are very close to Shah Muhammad, who wrote a *Jangnama* of the first Anglo-Sikh War in Punjabi in the popular meter of *Baint*. Shah Muhammad glorified the ideal of communal harmony (*'razi bahut rhede...'* i.e. they live in agreement and peace... Musalman, Hindu) and this was the reason behind the popularity of his work. After one hundred years of colonisation, Khushwant tried to revive this memory of communal peace in his writing.

The majority of works on the Sikh history suffer from treating the subject without a broad context. These works very often give the impression of being 'of the Sikhs, by the Sikhs, for the Sikhs.' It seems that they see Sikhs living in a completely hostile world in which the characters are flat and events are simple, predictable and one-dimensional. These works are more historical romances than works of history itself. But Khushwant adopted an altogether different approach. He provided full and necessary context to events which were sometimes more dominated by Mughals, Afghans, Rohillas, Marathas and British than the Sikhs themselves.

Khushwant did not believe in hiding the limitations of the historical Sikh personalities. He was honest in admitting their follies, and the limitations of their characters get sufficient treatment in his writings. He was not there to write a *Ramayana* or a *Mahabharata* of the Sikhs. He created a fine balance between glory and reality of the historical events. What made the book very popular with foreign audience was its lucid style, flowing narrative and intimate description of the subject. This book was, and so far is, the only popular introduction of Sikhism to the English speaking world.

An honest historian

Along with writing his book, *A History of Sikhs*, Khushwant devoted his energy to writing about Maharaja Ranjit Singh and his Lahore kingdom. Before these writings, the English speaking readers came to know about Maharaja Ranjit Singh, and his Lahore kingdom, either from the accounts of European visitors or from some narrow and drab academic (PhD) studies. Gurmukhi readership had access to some better writers, like Baba Prem Singh Hoti and Sohan Singh Sital, but the element of bias could not be ruled out, because these writers were mainly writing about Maharaja Ranjit Singh's achievement as a Sikh achievement, and the fall of his (Lahore) kingdom was seen as a conspiracy against the Sikhs. Khushwant's writings on Ranjit Singh in his books, *Ranjit Singh: Maharaja of Punjab* (1963) and *Sikh Kingdom: How the Sikhs Lost Their Kingdom* (1996), filled a big void of popular historical writings on Punjab in the 19th Century. Khushwant's trademark objectivity was at its best in these writings. While pointing one finger towards 'others', Khushwant pointed three fingers towards those people whom he portrayed.

The best thing about these books was that one could pick and read them without a sense of any heavy feeling that one usually feels with a book on the subject of history. In this case, he combined his research with his skills as a journalist and as a writer of fiction. His research showed that he was handling a lot of complex material, ranging from primary archival sources to secondary sources in Persian, English and Gurmukhi. The English side of the story was portrayed through using personal papers of British imperialists. None of his characters were painted on larger than life size canvas.

The story of the loss of the Sikh kingdom was akin to a Greek tragedy set in 19th Century Lahore. Khushwant captured it in the form of a story of faith, valour, deceit and pain. His objectivity did not dilute with the fact that his heart felt real pain for the loss of the Lahore kingdom.

His work on historical subjects was setting the trend in Indian popular historical writing, something later enriched by William Dalrymple. After its recent disillusionment with Saudi Arabianisation, the Pakistani media and intellectual class has started taking Punjabiat and Maharaja Ranjit Singh, and Lahore Kingdom much more seriously than earlier. A Pakistan journalist, Mubashir Luqman, called him the greatest ruler Lahore had ever seen. Many Pakistanis now seem to be looking towards the erstwhile rule of Maharaja Ranjit Singh as a role model of leadership that Pakistan should now look towards. In this case, Khushwant's writings become more relevant with the passage of time because there is no other book that can establish such instant connection between the young intellectuals and the memory of Maharaja Ranjit Singh. When a Pakistani Journalist, Zuabir Qureshi, read Khushwant's book, *Ranjit Singh: Maharaja of Punjab*, he felt so overwhelmed (in his words) that he translated it into Urdu and then published the Urdu version of the book in January 2015. If Pakistan looks towards Maharaja Ranjit Singh as a son of the soil, the credit goes to Khushwant Singh, another son of the soil.**

A humanitarian faith

Khushwant was unrelenting in his opposition to Khalistan and untiring in his books and writings on presenting a true picture of the Sikh history and the Sikh faith. But above all, he spoke as a Sikh for all the Sikhs who lived and worked in India and the world, and not only for the people living in Punjab. He saw Sikhism in all its beauty as a humanitarian faith, which had been preached by Guru Nanak and his successors as a reform to the wrong practices into which Hinduism seem to have fallen. He saw it as a faith that had emerged at a time of great conflict between Hindus and Muslims. It was also a time when the *Bhakti* movement was at its height in many parts of India and, in this moment, the entire emphasis was on moving away from Brahminical ritual and control and, instead, on worshipping God through devotion.

** Amanpreet Singh Gill has authored a book *'Non-Congress Politics in Punjab'*. He teaches Political Science at Sri Guru Tegh Bahadar Khalsa College, North Campus, Delhi University.

He wrote: 'Sikhism was born out of Hinduism. All ten Sikh Gurus were Hindus until they became Sikhs. The *Granth Sahib*, which Sikhs regard as the living light of the Gurus, can be described as the essence of *Vedas*. Nevertheless, like other reformist movements, Sikhism broke away from its parent Hindu body and developed its own distinct rites of worship and ritual, its own code of ethics, and its separate traditions, which cumulatively give it a distinct religious personality. The founder of the Sikh faith, Guru Nanak (1469-1539) was a Kshatriya of the caste of Bedis (those who know the Vedas)...He had a mystic experience after which he announced his mission with a simple statement: 'There is no Hindu, there is no mussalman'

It was essentially a simple faith, which preached the oneness of all mankind, a society without high and low, without caste and one in which the idea of service was paramount. The only commandments were to: work, give in charity, and take the name of God. There were no difficult Sanskrit verses to be chanted. So there was no need for priests if people had to worship. Instead, Guru Nanak, and the other Gurus who followed, all composed their own hymns in praise of God and nature, and among them were also the hymns of Muslims, lower caste weavers and Hindu minstrels and singers. It was a religion Khushwant found close to his heart even though he did not essentially believe in religion. He felt that Sikhism taught an essential humanity, which was certainly common, though in different forms, to other religions. But Sikhism being a modern religion, hardly 500 years old, had simplified the cloying ritual, the rigid doctrine and the strict observances that existed in the older religions.

All this would amply explain his virulent opposition to moments like Khalistan, which he saw as a threat to the secular existence of India. Though he was in a continuous conflict with the supporters of Khalistan and, for almost 20 years of his life, he had to be under threats, as well as find his way through the vortex of Sikh politics, Khushwant found a great amount of popularity and approbation among secular and right minded Sikhs everywhere. The hotheads and the gullible rustic people of Punjab, who were led away by the militant and aggressive tactics of leaders, like Bhindranwale, were of a fringe section. The vast majority of Sikhs in India and the world, engaged in professions, industry and businesses, writers and millable rustic people of Punjab were led away by the militant and aggressive Sikhs from the real significance of Sikhism.

He had started his writing career with the English translations of the verses of Guru Nanak from the *Japji Sahib*. He may not have believed in God as per his own assertion, but there must have been some empathy with the longing for spiritual elevation that made him so sensitive and deeply interested in the verses of the Sikh Scriptures. In a verse from the morning prayer of the Japji Sahib, Khushwant renders these lines written by Guru Nanak into English:

Before time itself, there was truth;
when time began to run its course,
He was the truth. Even now, He is the truth
and ever more shall the truth prevail.
Not by thought alone
can He be known, though one think
100,000 times, not in solemn silence,
nor are in deep meditation.
Though fasting yields an abundance of virtue,
it cannot appease the hunger for truth
no by none of these…
By Him are all forms created
by Him infused with life and blessed
by Him are some to excellence elated,
others born lonely and depressed.
Why is that it some have pleasure, others pain
by His Grace some are saved, others doomed to die.
His will encompass all there be, none beside.
O Nanak, he who knows has no ego.

A man of surprises, scholarship and impromptu jokes

Soli Sorabjee and friends remember...

The public image of Khushwant fades instantly as one gets to talk to his friends, most of them classified as the 'morningers'—people who stayed away from his public functions, his evening soirees and his book launches, which he loved so much. He had been known to say, though his latest book launch happened at home when he was 98 years old, that he would go to a book launch even on a stretcher. People close to him had a warm and indulgent affection for him. Most were people who had known him for decades. That in itself is interesting because the new friends and acquaintances were legions, but they came and went. It was only a few who really mattered and most of them had passed on before him; but to the few, who had remained, he was a warm and easy going friend. It did not matter if they did not meet very often. In most cases, they did not, because Khushwant was always busy with his writing or his social commitments. But the friendship was as fresh as ever.

Speaking on a television programme, David Davidar, the publisher, who had known the writer from his early days in publishing; and well-known historian and columnist, Ram Chander Guha, who admired Khushwant but strongly criticised his support to the Emergency, both said that perhaps the one great quality that distinguished Khushwant was his tremendous generosity. It came from his natural simplicity and kindness, and it was a quality that has been spoken about by innumerable people with whom he was friendly or whom he had helped on their way to journalism and writing. The story is told that Khushwant was a good friend of Nirad C Chaudhary, who way back in the early 60s had lived in financially strained circumstances. Khushwant himself was a struggling writer then. At that time, Khushwant gifted a typewriter to Nirad, saying that he needed one very badly. He had often said that: 'Nirad is one of the best Indian writers of English prose that we have."

Soli Sorabji: 'Calling a spade a spade'

One of his old friends from the 60s, when Khushwant was editor of the weekly, was Soli Sorabjee, a former

Advocate General of India and a legal luminary. He has been brilliant in his profession and also has a good sense of humour. One of his great interests has been listening to encouraging jazz music. Soli for long has been one of the guiding lights in the yearly performances of the *Jazz Yatra*, a coming together of modern jazz musicians from all over the world to perform in Indian cities.

Soli Sorabjee recalls: 'I met Khushwant Singh in the office of *The Illustrated Weekly of India* while he was editing it. I understand that, when he was asked to take over as its editor, the owners- the Jains, wanted him to go all out and so gave him a free hand to do his job, which was to boost the circulation of the magazine. My meeting was limited to saying hello to him and to give him my write-up for printing. I was a columnist writing every week. But it took us time to understand each other over a period of time, when the official 'hello hi' converted into friendship and we became lifelong friends.

We met often and discussed everything under the sun. Barring once, when he came to my residence for dinner with the clear understanding that the dinner should be served by 8pm- our frequent meetings took place at his residence at Sujan Singh Park. During the meetings, he would crack jokes and laugh. One thing about him that drew my attention was that he loved to tell jokes about the Sikhs unlike others, who frowned at such jokes, as it amounted to running down the

Sikh Community. He would not mind calling a spade a spade and when Maneka Gandhi moved the Delhi High Court to complain against Khushwant for making derogatory remarks against her, when she was thrown out of her Race Course Road residence by the then Prime Minister Mrs Indira Gandhi, I represented Khushwant in the High Court. He had a number of cases in the other courts as well. But he was never bothered about them.

I was one of the few privileged friends who were allowed to stay in his house at Kasauli. I used this privilege twice a year for many years. It is a delightful place and it felt much better if he also happened to be there.

Khushwant was a proud Sikh and would visit the Bangla Sahib gurdwara at night to escape the attention of devotees. Mind you he was not an atheist. At best, he was an agnostic. He visited the gurdwara a few weeks before his death.

He defended both the imposition of Emergency and Sanjay Gandhi's family planning. I endorsed family planning but not the manner in which it was implemented. Forced family planning violated fundamental rights of the Indian citizens and I told this to him.

Yes, Khushwant Singh was a barrister and I was also an advocate, but that does not mean that we became friends because of the profession. He taught corporate law at a law faculty in Pakistan (in his early days), but after a few years, he resigned from his job and headed for trying his hand at other things, until he finally found his destiny.

Coming back to our friendship, Khushwant had a different viewpoint about the profession and advocates. He felt that advocates were not lawyers, but liars. He was convinced that the judiciary was actually running the country. I tried to explain to him that this was not correct, but he just would not buy the argument. I came to Delhi in 1977 and was appointed law officer and, hence, it became important that the two of us meet more often.

He was a fearless journalist. He was free and frank, and wrote what he thought was correct. He had participated in a demonstration against the gagging of the media despite the fact that he had supported imposition of internal Emergency.'

Enjoyed meals with jokes

'Khushwant was pleased when I offered him *Dhanshak*, a typical Parsi dish.This traditional high protein dish (like chicken curry)is a perfect weekday supper to warm you up. If you do not fancy rice, you could serve this curry with wholemeal flat bread or roti or salad. While he enjoyed his meal, he would not stop himself telling the Santa Banta jokes. He was absolutely engrossed in writing the first draft of his famous Malice column and would not tolerate any interference by anyone. After he had an early lunch and nap, he would sit down with his legs on a *moorah* and revise his earlier draft, and make corrections. He used a pen to do his work. The column would be sent only after he was totally satisfied with the language, commas, full stops and contents. He was so meticulous.

After *Train to Pakistan*, which made him a celebrity overnight, his short stories and the novel, I shall not hear the nightingale, as far I am concerned, were decidedly his best works. Even at the age of 98, he was still producing books.

I have said earlier that Khushwant believed in his religion. His translations of *Sukhmani Sahib* and hymns from the *Guru Granth Sahib*, my Sikh friends tell me, more than proves his faith in religion and the translations were perfect. He believed in helping young budding journalists. He never spoke against someone behind his back, which means he did not believe in bitching. He was a good-hearted natural person.'

Charanjit Singh: A rare intellectual

Among his close family friends were the late Charanjit Singh, the owner of Campa Cola, and his wife, Harjeet, who took over the working of Le Meridien Hotel after her husband's passing away. He remained a good friend of the family. She often called on Khushwant, who had been inducted in the board of directors by her late husband. 'Call up Harjeet', Khushwant would tell his daughter, Mala, or his son, Rahul Singh, whenever he invited guests at his house for dinner. Apart from that, Charnjit Singh would make a halt at his residence in the mid-mornings to discuss policy issues and seek his guidance.

In Harjeet's words: 'My in-laws and Khushwant Ji's parents were close friends. Twice a week, my mother-in-law used to visit them and take me along for coffee. I used to enjoy going there and never used to get bored. Mr Khushwant Singh was not living there at that time. I first met him in 1968/69 at a function, where he was a speaker, and I was very impressed. My husband, Mr Charanjit Singh, had gone to see him during the riots and, on his return, he told me about him. I was keen on meeting him personally. He used to listen to Kirtan, while sipping at his glass of whiskey. My husband once asked him about this strange combination and Khushwant Ji laughingly replied, 'We can understand Kirtan better this way.'

In 1984, I met Khushwant Ji with my husband. He cracked many jokes, which I enjoyed. He said that he wanted to hear jokes from me. He wrote a few of my jokes in his column also. I was really very keen on hearing and exchanging jokes with him and that's how I became very close and friendly with him. In any parties, which took place in his house, we were the first ones on his invitees list. I was lucky to be there for all the parties and met many dignitaries, such as then Prime Minister Dr Manmohan Singh and President Dr Abdul Kalam, many ambassadors, ministers, and many celebrities, including Jayalalithaa, Javed Akhtar and Shabana Azmi.

I have a farmhouse where Khushwant Ji used to regularly go and write his books. Every morning, around 11am, he used to go there. On weekends, my husband and I used to go to the farmhouse. Both Mrs and Mr Khushwant Singh used to join us. He used to tell me about the calls of the birds and would even tell me about the names of the birds only on hearing their chirping.

When my husband wanted him to join our hotel's board of directors, he said 'I am not aware of any business management or financial management. What will I do? But if you still want me to be with you, I will certainly join.' It was a great honour to have him with us. When my husband passed away, he was the first to visit me and supported me.

He was the one who convinced me to take over. I was not very keen on involving myself in the business, though I was on the Board. I knew the business dealings well and I am happy that I took over. Mr Khushwant Singh wanted me to visit him daily and let him know what was happening in the office. He used to guide and encourage me.

He never believed in God. But he used to hear Kirtan and his translation of *Japji Sahib* is amazing. He never believed in *Bhog* or any other rituals after death. He was a rare kind of intellectual, a great writer and a noble soul.

He was very fond of the Amaltas tree. When he stopped

going anywhere, he often used to enquire if it is in full bloom during the season. I used to visit him every second day while coming to office and many a time he used to say, 'My end is coming soon.'

Yes, I do feel a vacuum after his death. Ever since his death, I did not go to Sujan Singh Park. Whenever I pass through that place, I still feel that he is there. I have such lovely memories of him and I feel happy about it. I think I am blessed that I had him as a good friend and guide, who was a big support after my husband's death.'

Arpana Caur: A precious heart

Arpana Caur is one of India's best known artists. She has exhibited her works at major art events all over the world. Her works are also on display at the National Gallery of Modern Art in Delhi. She has done some important work on women and the girl child. Her series of paintings on Hymns of the Gurus has found wide acclaim for their quality and portrayal of the message on peace and spirituality. One of her paintings of Guru Nanak hung just above the chair on which Khushwant would habitually sit in his house.

In Arpana's words: 'Khushwant Uncle had friendship of four decades with my mother (Ajeet Caur, a Punjabi writer, featured in the last section of this book). She made him the president of her academy and consulted him frequently. I knew he loved us and missed us when there were long gaps in our visits. Every two to three months, he and Kawal Aunty came to our house for a meal and the bones were always taken away for his cats, never once did he forget them.

Such was his generosity that, many years ago, when he heard I was exhibiting in Bombay for the first time, he quietly shot off letters to all the journalists he knew (Busybee, Sobha De etc.) informing them that Arpana, who was like his daughter, was having an exhibition. I would then find an avalanche of write-ups on my exhibition, including a cover story in the *Bombay* magazine.

In those days, coverage for the arts was otherwise so scanty that, in many cases, I would not receive any feedback on my show till one of those journalists would write on it or tell me. At the release of *Hymns of the Sikh Gurus* at the Le Meridien hotel,years ago, he shouted from the stage, 'Call her, she must be hiding at the back; this is her book, not mine.' That was the kind of grace he was endowed with. Two feet above his head (while sitting on his usual working chair) hung the painting of Nanak that Mala had asked me to do for his surprise birthday present.

When he breathed his last, he lay perfectly peacefully, with his usual glow and innocence. And, as I lifted his head from his pillow for the last turban to be tied, I knew that was one of the most precious heads (and hearts) of our century. Never will I be able to pass Sujan Singh Park easily without a void in my heart.'

Bobby Bedi: He never interfered in the making of the film on *Train to Pakistan*

Bobby Bedi shot to fame when he produced the film, *Bandit Queen,* based on the life of a notorious woman dacoit, Phoolan Devi. The film was directed by Shekhar Kapoor. In 1989, he teamed up with Pamela Rooks to make a film on Khushwant's novel, *Train to Pakistan*.

Recalling the shooting of the film, which took place near Chandigarh, Bobby Bedi said: 'It must be mentioned that Khushwant did not interfere during the shooting or visit the sets while the shooting was in progress. Once the film was ready, he appreciated the efforts of all and complimented us for doing our best.' But he did not look totally happy with the kind and the quality of the film. 'The film could have been a great commercial film,with the kind of budget required in the region of 80 crore plus. I feel like I could re-do the film myself,' he said.

Mohan Agashe, a celebrated actor, who played the role of district magistrate in the film, said that Khushwant Ji was very impressed with his performance, as he complimented him: You have done much better than any other actor who may have been picked up for the job.

'If you don't drink, don't come in the evening'

Recalling his meetings and interviews with Khushwant, veteran journalist and co-author of this work, Onkar Singh, writes: 'I must admit that Khushwant Singh Ji was fond of me and he would spend more than half an hour on each occasion I went to see him. He was a bit upset when I first went to see him in the mid-eighties, as I had no prior appointment at that time and yet managed to gate-crash to meet him.'

In Onkar Singh's words: 'Once I phoned him to ask if I could come and see him in the evening. He said I was welcome and that I could share a drink with him. "But, Sir, I don't drink", I said. For a moment, I thought he was nonplussed at the fact that a Sardar did not drink. But his reply took me by surprise, as he said: "In that case, don't show up when I am having drinks."

After one of our meetings, as I was about to take my leave, Khushwant led me to a room where books were placed everywhere on the racks. "I have too many books. Take as many as you can carry," he said. Then he gave me a personal copy of his book, *A History of Sikhs*. "Read it", he told me. I took some of the books and was quite elated that the great Khushwant had given me his books. He was in his 90s at that time and had become a little hard of hearing. But he did not like to wear his hearing aid at all times. Sometimes, when I asked him questions, he would tell me to write them down on a piece of paper and then he would reply. It had been a long time since I had first met him and, in a way, it was sad to see him lose some of his faculties. I had met him a number of times during my carrier as a journalist and, though all our meetings were only for interviews, I had begun to admire his tenacity and determination in continuing to write.'"

Amapreet Singh Gill: A compliment from Khushwant

In 2010, I received a compliment from Khushwant on my research on the Sikh warrior, Baba Banda Singh Bahadar, which was published in *Nishaan*. Its editor, Pushpinder Singh Chopra, communicated this to me. I had dug a bit deeper into *Gurmukhi* sources on Baba Banda Singh Bahadar and discovered some facts, which Khushwant found interesting. In 2011, Pushpinder Singh brought out Delhi of Sikhs, a special issue of *Nishaan*, and I happened to be its sole author along with one piece by Khushwant. Pushpinder was my ticket to the legendary world of Khushwant's house.

Right on the door was a Ganesh idol, which had seen celebrities like Zeenat Amaan, Rajiv Gandhi and many others being shown the door at 8 pm, which was the curfew time during the evenings at Khushwant's house. I was lucky that Rahul Singh opened the door. He told me that Khushwant had declined to see a BBC team earlier in the afternoon.

During my discussion with Khushwant, I found that his memory was intact at the age of 96. He narrated to me passages from Captain Amarinder Singh's *The Last Sunset:*

The Rise and Fall of Lahore Darbar (2010). Only his hearing had failed him. While struggling with his hearing aid, he lamented in Punjabi: 'Jeon da koi swad nahin riha,' (there is no fun now in living). He was writing something and he asked me the third line after *Gagan Damama Bajio* (by poet Kabir). He would not hear my low voice and I tried to explain twice or more. Finally, he gave me his black pen and an envelope to write it down and asked, 'Gurmukhi vich likh deo.' When I was writing the third line, I realized that I was writing with Khushwant's pen; and I was writing about Kabir's words on the warrior who was there to take up the challenge. For me, Khushwant was a warrior, with a pen in his hand, an old warrior whose time was almost up, but battle was not over.'

Jinnah—Father of Pakistan, but a Son of India

One of Khushwant's old friends from Pakistan was Fakir S. Aijazuddin, a successful chartered accountant, but also well known for his books on the history of art. He last met Khushwant on 4 March 2014, just a fortnight before Khushwant passed away on 20 March 2014. Aijazuddin had known Khushwant for over 30 years and, according to him, Khushwant regarded his birth village of Hadali (now in Pakistan) with great affection. At this meeting, Khushwant said to him: 'I have told them I want to be buried in Hadali.'

Aijazuddin had made it a practice to visit Khushwant

whenever he was in Delhi. This time it was to present him his new book. However, he could not meet him on the first day, as Khushwant was resting. On the next day, with daughter Mala's help, he met Khushwant, who was basking outside his home in the sun at that time. Khushwant was 99 years old at that time but he still recognised his old friend immediately. Aijazuddin gave him his book "Inscribe it for me,' Khushwant said. Once this was done. He said again, 'Now, write it in order to.' Looking at the book, Khushwant recited a couplet of Iqbal.

'You know that I am 99 years old,' Khushwant said.

'May my years be added to yours,' said Aijazuddin, who recounts: 'He looked up at me with the softest expression' and said, 'No, but may you live as long as I have."

It was a precious and a sad moment, as Aijazuddin recalls: 'I held his hand, the hand that had spent a lifetime writing books and inimitable articles, and I kissed it. He brushed his cheek with mine. Both of us knew that it was a farewell. I left and stood on the Greville outside, recalling our first meeting on 21 August 1978.'

That meeting had taken place when Aijazuddin had visited Khushwant to show him his first book, *Pahari Paintings and Sikh Portraits in the Lahore Museum*. At that time, Khushwant had given him his book, *Fall of the Kingdom of the Punjab.* According to Aijazuddin, Khushwant's academic achievements were the most prominent part of his life. He felt that his more popular works, such as the articles, short stories, novels and his jokes, gained him more fame and fortune, and 'certainly notoriety, but none yielded him the state that I believe he deserved as a serious writer.'

Aijazuddin also recalled the time when, on one occasion, Khushwant stunned his Pakistani audience during a memorial lecture for his friend, Manzur Qadir. This was at Lahore in 1989. Khushwant declared that, before Jinnah became the Father of Pakistan, he was the Son of India. The audience was completely silent at this remark. Aijazuddin adds: 'No one but Khushwant Singh would have shown such locative mysteriousness and no one else would have been able to calm and then conciliate his audience with a fire extinguishing speech that followed.'

One from the heart for a man with all heart

Bhola Badshah

A well-known Punjabi writer, Ajeet Caur, who was a good friend of Khushwant for over four decades, shares her following memories of the writer. She has nine collections of short stories and two novels to her credit, translated into many Indian languages. She has received awards and honours from literary organisations and was honoured with the Academy Award in 1985 for her autobiography, *Khana Badosh*. She is the mother of the famous artist, Arpana Caur.

The Hindi word 'bhola' means innocent or 'simple' in English. That is not what one would think of Khushwant, whose public image is far from one of innocence. And yet, it is significant that almost all his close friends, who have survived him or those whom we have met during his earlier times, have said that Khushwant had a childlike and trusting quality. He has been called a 'loveable child-man' and a 'mischievous fellow'. Those who knew him well steered clear of his public image, met him when he was alone and not surrounded by people, and cherished his serious and sensitive side.

In Ajeet Caur's words:

'My friendship with Khushwant matured over the years after this interview, and he was very close to me and my daughter, Arpana, whom he entrusted to make paintings for his book, *Songs of the Gurus*. Arpana did another set for his daughter Mala's book, *Nanak the Guru*. He was very fond of her, and it was she who wrapped a saffron patka, a simple form of the turban, on his head before his body was taken for cremation in March 2014.

Songs of fishermen and a nightingale

During an interview with me, he walked down the memory lane:

'I was in Italy, driving on the highway along Lake Garda...It was at the peak of summer. The metallic grey road seemed to be melting under the fury of a scorching sun. My throat was parched with thirst. Bewildered by the harsh sun and the furnace-like wind, I was looking for a hotel.

I looked into all the hotels on the highway, in every city

and every town. But it was the tourist season. No room was available in any hotel. I felt I was going out of my mind in that searing heat. I was tired and thirsty. Moving from town to town, I began to feel there wasn't a cool corner for me in the whole wide world. The road then wound itself towards a lake. I also turned my car onto that road. The road was absolutely forlorn, I couldn't see anybody or anything along the way. The road continued over the middle of the lake. I had expected a rush of cool breeze from the water, but there was none. The water of the lake was scalding.

My breath was suffocated inside my ribcage, as if I was swallowing oven-fresh choking sand. I felt my lungs had themselves become the open furnace of an ironsmith! The car moved on for six or seven kilometres. And then came a tiny island: San Sirmione, with low hillocks, a few houses of fishermen, and a small hotel. The hotel looked almost uninhabited. I got a room there. I took my bath and freshened up. I peeped outside my window. Dusk was descending. The oven-hot air was mellowing. Outside the hotel, there were huge trees, dense and heavy, with green leaves. I moved towards those trees.

I was exhausted. I lay down under a fir tree. The dense shade of the tree, the soft breeze caressing my body, soft music of the gentle lapping of waves of the lake, the melting grey sky, I don't know when I dozed off.I don't know how long I slept. But suddenly, my sleep was shattered by a dazzling light. I got up and looked upwards. From across the foliage of the fir tree, the full moon was pouring its silvery light on me. Dazzling white light was being showered over me. Intensely white!

Perched on a branch of the tree, a nightingale was singing in intoxication!

The fishermen were coming home. Happy with the weight of the fish caught during the day. Somebody was playing a guitar. Many fishermen were singing. Their melodious voices mingled with the lyrical music of the waves of the lake.

From the jet dark sky, the stars were looking down at me. Me, a stranger! But I didn't feel like a stranger there. I felt as if I was born there. Under the huge trees, and on the banks of this lake, it was as if I had been playing as a toddler, and growing up. And today, I was also a fisherman, returning home with my catch, intoxicated with the day-long labour, which yielded a huge haul of fish.

The moon was shining only for me. The stars were looking only at me. The nightingale was singing only for me. And under the moonlight, the waves of the lake were passionately awaiting my touch like a beloved longing for my caress.

Perhaps I was not thinking about anything. The magic of that moment had sunk into me. I had left my body and was feeling one with the soft air, floating in it. I don't know what God is. I don't know what is outside the existence of the body. But in that moment, I stepped out of my body and merged with something intoxicating and soft.

A feeling of infinite space ! Strange and other-worldly! I could feel intensely every needle-like leaf of the fir-trees, and every dancing wave of the lake as the extension of my own sensations. I was on the other side of consciousness. Dumb in the presence of so much beauty! I couldn't even move a finger. I was in an absolute trance, half-conscious and intoxicated!'

And he fell silent.I looked at his face. He was still strolling down the memory lane.

Can you recognize this man? He was the one everybody called a scoundrel and womaniser. The King of Sleaze! They say he couldn't think beyond nude women. 'Dirty Old Man', they called him.This is Khushwant Singh. I call him 'The Khushwant Singh'. In the whole wide world, there cannot be any other Khushwant.The one and the only Khushwant Singh.

I met him for the first time at a small party, a few decades ago. Satindar Singh, a journalist, who worked for *The Economic Times* introduced us. He loved being called Sati and was a brilliant historian. 'Come home sometime', Khushwant said, with his usual large-hearted and affectionate smile.

A year prior to this, he had edited an anthology of

Punjabi short stories, and had not included my story in it. I thought I should retort: 'If you don't like my stories, why should I come to your place?' But then I gave him the benefit of doubt that of being unfamiliar with my writings. After all, he was not a Punjabi writer. He himself had said that English was his mother tongue. So I granted him the concession of ignorance, and chose to be immensely flattered by his invitation. Who wouldn't? It was no joke to be invited by the great writer and editor, Khushwant Singh.

I called him after a couple of days. He said, 'Seven in the evening'. I was there at 7 pm. He was sprawled in an easy chair, his legs resting on a moderately high moorhs, a cane stool. He was sitting in the right hand corner of the room-and the spotlight of my memory is focused on him. There were a couple of his other friends too, and everybody was sipping whiskey from elegant cut-glasses. Khushwant was the king in that gathering. He had a royal aura around him. Dressed in loosely hanging Pathani salwar and kurta, and a carelessly wrapped loose turban, he seemed to be lording over everyone.

Khushwant was different

Another day, another meeting on his invitation! The time allotted was 11 am. When I entered his room, he was reading a tightly printed, small-sized *Guru Granth Sahib*, the holy book of the Sikhs, and was marking the lines and words with his pencil. On the other table, there was a glass of garnet coloured drink. As I was not familiar with drinks, I cannot tell what drink it was.

He asked me, 'Will you have rum?' I replied, 'I haven't yet learnt to drink any hard stuff." He offered me a gin-and-lime, and said this was not a hard drink. 'It is very soft', he insisted. I could feel myself blushing. It was not easy to confess that I had not touched a drop of any hard drink till then.

'If you haven't learnt to drink, how do you write then? And I confess you have a powerful pen. I have read two of your books of short stories. Superb!' he commented.

I must have blushed some more! Khushwant Singh himself was admiring my writings! What more could any writer expect from life? I was carried away by his admiration.

Usually, people who have attained Khushwant Singh's status, wear a hundred masks. They feel they are standing at the top of the Everest, looking down on millions of crawling creatures. Khushwant was different. Like a soft breeze wandering in forests, carrying the fragrance of trees and flowers on its wings, moving and flying like butterflies.

I was ready to fall in love with him. After all, he had several love affairs in his life. But I am sure, in all these affairs, the women must have taken the initiative, and poor Khushwant must have agreed to be seduced by them, and tolerate the affairs. In our case, I was a very shy person. So there was no scope of his getting seduced by me. Our friendship lasted for several decades without any romantic undertones.

Falling in love and friendships

I asked him once, 'How many times have you fallen in love?' He smiled, 'Innumerable times. At various places, in different cities and countries. Not like Punjabi poets, who are convinced that a love affair is only a once-in-a-lifetime affair, and is carried on even in the next birth, if there is any!'

I said 'Have you forgotten? I am not a poet; I am a story-teller.' 'But you write in Punjabi', he commented.

'Why are you so sceptical about Punjabi?' I asked.

'Punjabi ...' and he sighed sarcastically.

'Do you like any Punjabi writer?' I asked further.

'No,only the poetry of Guru Nanak', he said.

I happened to be in Bombay when he was at the weekly. I had thought of calling him, taking an appointment, and meeting him in his office the next day.It was about 5.30 pm. I was going towards a gallery,and suddenly I saw him strolling in the corridor of Feroz Shah Mehta Road.The corridor was crowded over with small little shops and people.

He ambled like an elephant in a jungle.Baggy trousers, an equally baggy tee-shirt, carelessly wrapped turban. I still remember its colour;it was light maroon. He carried his umbrella on his shoulder like a farmer carrying his tools. He met me with great affection and wasa little dazzled by my unexpected presence in that corridor verandah. I felt transported into the cozy sunlight after a bath in cold winter.

I asked about his family. He said, 'They are in Delhi'. I had seen his graceful wife, Kawal, taking walks in Lodhi Ga den. She always wore a salwar and an umbrella-cut shirt, plain from the top, but umbrella-cut from waist down. She got her clothes stitched from the same tailor, who had a small little shop in Hotel Ambassador, very close to Khushwant's house, a part of Sujan Singh Park. This Sujan Singh Park was built by Sir Sobha Singh, Khushwant's father, who named it after his own father's name Sujan Singh, Khushwant's grandfather.

When Khushwant was allotted a bungalow in Lodhi Estate as Member of the Rajya Sabha, Kawal gave it to her tailor for five years to stay there, during Khushwant's tenure of Rajya Sabha. She not only looked like a maharani, she had the heart of a queen.

Khushwant said he met her in London. He said, 'She was the most beautiful Indian girl around. Half the Indian boys in London were crazy about her. I was dazzled by her beauty! Now it had become a matter of honour for me. I had to win her from all those boys. So I got married to her'.

The unwanted carpet

Kawal was a very strong woman. Whatever she ordered had to be done. She just said it once, and Khushwant melted and yielded to her 'order'. She had something regal and queenly about her. That is how she had tamed this unusually talented man.

Khushwant has confessed: 'She is very strict. Particularly about the quantity of alcohol I drink, and the time I go to bed and wake up. She is strict with all the people who come to see me, and all those who invite us home. She doesn't allow anyone to overstay for a minute. She claps and says, 'Time to leave'. And everybody leaves like obedient lambs. Nobody minds her diktat, which from anybody else would be taken as rude. She has that authoritative voice, which everybody obeys without feeling insulted. If she hadn't been such a strict disciplinarian, I could never have accomplished what I have.

Wherever we go, she tells the hosts that we will have our dinner at exact eight, and will leave before nine. It is because of her discipline that I sleep early, and get up early the next morning and start my work. My work, my walks, my health, my achievements, all the books I have written, all are indebted to this Sardarni's discipline.'

I realize that Kawal was a very lucky woman because her husband admired her even in her absence. I really came to know her one evening at a diplomat's house. Both of them were there, Khushwant and Kawal. Khushwant was sad about his departure from the weekly and was reviving his old contacts, who had been waiting for Khushwant's return to Delhi. I said, 'Now that you are a little free, why don't you drop in at my place for dinner? Let us celebrate your relaxed break from hectic work.'

'When?' Khushwant asked, with his usual generous smile.

'Whenever you feel like, but let's decide about the day just now. Because this is not one of your Amritsari invitations', I reminded to him what he usually said about casual invitations which are never serious.

'What about this Saturday then?' he asked.

'Fine! Around seven then? Do bring Sardarni Sahiba also', I said. Kawal was sitting right next to Khushwant at that time, but talking with someone else to her right.

When Kawal looked at me, I told her, 'Saturday. Please come for dinner. Will you remember, or should I call you to remind you on Saturday morning?'

'Saturday? What for?' Kawal asked, looking puzzled.

'Khushwant has just chosen the day for dinner', I was bewildered.

'If he has accepted the invitation, let him go. I cannot come. And he is also bluffing you. Even he cannot come to you. Our Mala has a little daughter, and we have to baby-sit with her. She doesn't allow us to go anywhere in the evenings', Kawal explained.

She knew what she was doing to me, because she was there. I was so shattered that I just returned home and didn't stay over for dinner. Next day, Khushwant called me, 'No use feeling insulted. It is my Sardarni's style. You are stupid to feel hurt. If I tell you what happened the other day, you will realize you didn't get an iota of what she is capable of giving.'

An unwanted carpet

In Khushwant's words, 'The other day, Menaka Gandhi and her mother, Amteshwar, came to my home. You know, I am helping Menaka with her newly launched magazine, *Surya*; so they thought that, since I do not accept any remuneration, they should present me a costly gift. So they brought a large Persian carpet to our house. I was just soaking in their generosity, and then Sardarni came out of her room, saw that Persian carpet and shouted, 'Horrible! Who the hell has brought this obnoxious carpet?' Both Menaka and Amteshwar got very nervous. Even I did! Sardarni thundered, 'I don't like this horrible colour. This has no place in our home. Pick it up and get lost.' Amteshwar mumbled, 'We will change the colour', but Kawal retorted back, 'But pick this up first and take it out from here.'

Amiteshwar, really shuddering now, started rolling the carpet, and mumbled, 'Ask your servant to keep it in our car'. Sardarni thundered, 'I don't have any servants. Take it back the way you brought it in'. So Amiteshwar called her driver, and both of them carried the carpet outside; Menaka helped.

'This is what my Sardarni is capable of doing',

Khushwant was laughing, and I could see a trace of pride in his laughter. As if a mother is describing her wayward son, an only child who is spoiled to the limit.

Loyal to Mrs Gandhi

This episode took place during the Emergency period in the country. Indira Gandhi was the 'Supreme Empress' of her Kingdom. Even Chief Ministers, Governors and Ministers waited for hours to catch the eye of Sanjay Gandhi, or his wife Maneka. A smile from either of them could ensure them their fortune; and an indifferent, dismissive look meant that their boats had holes in their bottoms.

Those were the days when people felt being deceived by Khushwant, because he continued to write in favour of Indira Gandhi and the Emergency. He had a special soft corner for Sanjay Gandhi and his plans, which he implemented like Hitler. People commented, 'Why won't he write in favour of Indira Gandhi? After all, she is the Empress of the country, and Sanjay is her Prince-of-Wales, the heir apparent, the next Prime Minister of the country!'

And then, Indira Gandhi lost the elections.

Even the most ardent of her admirers started avoiding being seen in her proximity. They pretended that they were always against the Emergency and all the atrocities connected with it, and claimed they were silent because they were afraid for their own lives.I was thinking about Khushwant.

Knowing him, I was sure he would not compromise on his position. The next issue of the weekly confirmed that he was sticking to his stand, and was still glorifying Indira Gandhi.Friends appreciated his determination to stand by his ideas and his conviction, but the owners of Weekly didn't like it, and he was asked to put in his papers. He had to leave the weekly and return to Delhi, where he was appointed the editor of *The National Herald*. However, he did not stick to his new position, and left it like a wandering minstrel.

Some years later, he was editing *New Delhi*. My daughter had written a comprehensive research paper about women painters of the world. She wrote to the 'editor' of *New Delhi*, addressing him as 'Sir', and not as Khushwant Uncle, because whenever Khushwant came to our home, Arpana, in her usual style, would withdraw to her room and never participate in our get-togethers, so she had never met him before this incident. Even Khushwant's daughter, Mala, kept away from Khushwant's parties. In her letter, she had elaborated a little about her article, and had asked the editor if he would like to use it in *New Delhi*.

She got a reply within two days and was advised that she should immediately send her article to the *New Delhi* office.Arpana had forbidden me from letting Khushwant know that she was my daughter. So I kept quiet.The article was published. Arpana went to the *New Delhi* office to collect the pictures she had sent along with the article. Khushwant chatted with her about her interest in paintings, saying he would like to see some of them, and said, "You resemble your mother a lot." That was the man called Khushwant Singh.

Laughter like a mountain spring

And then he got one of the most prestigious positions in journalism. He was appointed the editor of the *Hindustan Times*. I called him. And he promptly said with open-hearted generosity, "Why don't you drop in at my office? Tomorrow? At five? Will it suit you?" Any time given by Khushwant suited me.The winter was waning away. The mid-day soft sunlight was pink and mild, and to meet with him, I walked through his office corridor, which ended at Khushwant's room, on the right side. It was still the age of typewriters. The age of computers was still not with us. I could hear the keyboards clicking from almost every room. And I felt as if I was wending my way forward in a beehive, towards the sanctum of the queen bee.

He got up from his chair and walked towards me. With his right arm, he gave me a casual hug. His hug, an expression of his whole personality! He said in a confidential whisper, 'Let us run away from here. Many people are pouring in to see me, and I want to be with you alone.' He collected the papers spread on his table and put them in a file. The file went into the drawer. And we walked out of his office. He was happy playing truant, as if he was a small boy who had run away from his school to play *gulli danda* with his friends in the open fields. He shared a joke with me about some of his unwanted visitors and laughed heartily.

"Khushwant, do your children also laugh like you, with so much gusto?" I asked.

Once he took me to Gaylord for a cup of tea. We had one sandwich each, and tea. When Khushwant saw the bill, he was crestfallen, "Isn't it plain loot? Just a sandwich each and tea, and the bill is eighteen rupees! Eighteen rupees !"

Once he bought a book from Ramakrishna bookshop. It was for about three hundred rupees. He signed the bill, and said, 'My salary for half a month is gone!' Though it was an exaggeration, he was really worried! Then he saw the publisher's title and got more worried, "Oh, it is an imprint of Oxford University Press! I could easily have saved a lot of discount because my son-in-law is looking after that publishing house."'

Some talk of history

Talking of Connaught Place, he said, 'All this was a dense forest then. It required great courage to buy land at even two rupees a yard. Daryaganj was the centre of Delhi. Modern School was also first started in Daryaganj. On this side of Daryaganj, it was all wilderness,forests of keekar mainly. You occasionally came across Gujjar taking out their cattle. Connaught Place started being constructed around 1920.'

Walking beside him, I always felt he was a big banyan tree.

'When my father got the Regal Cinema constructed, hardly four or five people came to see the films. We used to implore our friends and relatives, "Please come to see the film. It is free."If the audience was just four or five people, we had to beg them to go home and bring some friends the next day, so that the film could be screened.'

'The areas where you see Chawri Bazar and Hauz Kazi today, was the red light area. Very hesitantly, I sometimes went there out of curiosity, strolling with halting steps. I could see them all decked up on their balconies. I could hear the ankle bells, and the music of harmonium and tabla, and singing ascending to a crescendo.'

'Never went up any stairs', he laughed, 'no, never! But afterwards…it was a prostitute to whom I lost my virginity.'

'Here in Delhi?' I asked.

He replied: 'No, in Bombay. I went to Bombay by train, from Delhi and just got out of Victoria Station. She was very fat and ugly, a Punjaban. She called me. I went to her. How did I know that…? I was young and inexperienced. My beard hadn't yet grown. She took me to her room. I was almost frozen with fear and apprehension. Then I went to the UK and was there for a year. Nothing happened there. I was truly afraid of approaching or talking to any girl. And no girl took the first step to be involved with me. I came back as inexperienced as I was when I had left. Here, friends asked me a thousand questions. I had nothing to report, so I used to invent sexy episodes and narrate them to gain some respect among my friends. But I decided that this won't do any more. So when I went back after spending a month's holiday, I made good all my loss.'

Childhood amidst the sand dunes

When Khushwant talked of his childhood, he seemed like an innocent child. He used to play on the sand dunes of Hadali, his native village. The sound of the metallic bells around the necks of the camels fascinated him. Holding the edge of his grandmother's veil, he relished fresh butter with the left-over chapatti from the last night.

In his words: 'My younger brother, Daljit, still loves to eat stale chapatti and stale lentils. His liver is weak but still he cannot get rid of this luxury. One must change one's habits with advancing age.' Khushwant might have changed his eating habits with age, but his soul still loved the expanse of the sand dunes of Hadali, and the glamour of shimmering sands in the moonlit nights.

One day in 1976, Khushwant, Arpana and I were chatting in our Neeti Bagh house. I had not invited anyone else. We wanted to enjoy his presence all by ourselves.

I hadn't invited my father into the living room so that he was not disturbed by Khushwant's scotch. He was a devout

Sikh and believed all intoxicants were forbidden by the Gurus. He was reading something in his room. Khushwant moved from one painting to the other, all Arpana's paintings, and he made very profound comments. He liked them all. Suddenly he saw my father sitting in the open courtyard which was between Darji's (my father's) room and the living room. In the slowly descending grey dusk, Darji was sitting in his easy chair, enjoying the soft, gentle, quiet evening.

Khushwant strolled to my father and graciously wished him, 'Sat Siri Akal jee!'

Darji responded, 'Sat Siri Akal.'

'Why are you sitting here alone?' asked Khushwant.

'It was a bit hot in the room. It is very pleasant outside', Darji replied.

'From the way you speak, from your intonation, it seems you are from Sargodha', Khushwant smiled.

'Yes, I belong to Bhera. It was in Sargodha', Darji replied.

'I know that. I am also from that part, from Shahpur', Khushwant said.

'Shahpur?' Darji beamed.

'No, not exactly. There was a village called Hadali, in Shahpur District', Khushwant said.

'I know about Hadali. It was very near to our Bhera', Darji said.

Within a moment, they were talking like two long-lost friends, accidentally reunited.

'Please come in', Khushwant invited him into the living room.

'No, I will rather sit here in the open air. The whole day long one gets tired of the suffocating air from air-conditioners and fans. At this time of the day, at dusk, it is pleasant to sit outside and enjoy the fresh air', Darji turned down the invitation. Khushwant sailed back into the living room.

Darji asked me, 'Who is he?'I realized my blunder. I hadn't introduced them properly. I said, 'He is Khushwant Singh.'

'Hain? That Khushwant Singh?' Darji was really amazed.

'Yes, the same!' I told him.

Darji was still dazed, when I had to leave him to serve food.

With Darji, he had been talking about Hadali. Even after coming back to the living room, he was still in Hadali. "Our village Hadali was about thirty kilometres away from Jhelum, in the centre of Mithha Tiwana and Khushab.'

'Khushwant, when were you born?' Darji asked.

'On the papers, it is 2 February 1915. But my grandmother said that I was born in Bhadon. The monsoons had just been over. So I guess it must be the month of August', Khushwant explained.

'Did you grow up in Hadali? A small boy playing in the sand dunes of that small village?' Darji asked. And Khushwant explained:

'My grandfather had shifted here, to Delhi. His name was Sujan Singh. In Hadali, he was a very popular man, and very rich. A railway station was named after him: "Kot Sujan Singh". The other day Pakistan's Ambassador told me that they had not changed the name. It is still the same: "Kot Sujan Singh."

'My grandfather had been allotted large tracts of land, about two thousand acres, in between Montgomery and Khanewal, Mian Channu. The people of our area were very strong, robust, tall and handsome. They were of a mixed breed from Baluchistan and Punjab, very hard working and honest. Half of the Viceroy's bodyguards were picked up from my village. During the First Great War, my grandfather had persuaded many young men to enrol themselves in the British Army.

The British rulers felt indebted to my grandfather. So they allotted large areas of land to him. Lands were in the area where a large canal system was operative. The lands were very fertile, and the wheat was like gold nuggets. So my grandfather made several factories with the spare money. All poor and dishonest relatives were given jobs in those factories. He had just two son: one, my father, Shobha Singh; and the other, Ujjal Singh, who later became the Governor of Madras.'

He continued with Hadali: 'Once I wrote somewhere that my grandfather was a money lender. The whole family got furious with me, because it was wrong. They clarified that, before the lands were allotted to them, they were in business. They would load rock salt from the mines of Kheeora and bring it to Amritsar. After selling the salt in Amritsar, they would load the camels with cloth, candles, and a few fancy items and bring them back to the village. Afterwards, when lands came into their possession, they became big landlords and industrialists.'

'Why didn't you join the family business?' Darji continued his investigation, and Khushwant explained:

'I was still a toddler when my grandfather came to Delhi. Soon he sent for my father and eldest brother too. They too came to Delhi. I was left alone in Hadali with my grandmother. I remained there for about five years, I suppose. My grandmother was always busy doing something or the other, and kept reciting Gurbani all the time. In our village, almost all the houses belonged to Muslim families. There were only four or five Hindu-Sikh families in the village. There was no school in the village. So my grandmother made me recite first five stanzas of *Japji*. And when I was three years old, she sent me to the local gurudwara to learn *Gurmukhi* and read the Holy Scriptures from the Sikh priest of the gurudwara.'

'Who would believe today that this great writer and intellectual got his initial education in a village dharamsala!' Khushwant laughed.

'When did you start on your journey of creative writing?' Darji probed further.

'In Canada, my work, *A Story: Mark of Vishnu*, was published in Harpers literary magazine. I couldn't believe that the best literary magazine could print my story! That was the beginning. And then, there was no looking back. I kept writing. My first collection of short stories was published in 1950. The title of the book was the same: *Mark of Vishnu*. It got rave reviews.'

He continued: 'Kawal arrived with both our children to the UK to spend summer vacations. I resigned the same day. I had also paid six months' rent for my apartment, and had collected enough whiskey for my sustenance. I didn't bother about anything else. After resigning, I kept writing day and night. I wrote the first short history of the Sikhs. Allen and Unwin accepted it for publishing. The first draft of *Train to Pakistan* was written in London, but I finished it here, in Delhi. The first name of the novel was *Mano Majra*. Later it was changed to *Train to Pakistan*. I translated Japji also in London, and it was also published there.'

'Kept working only? Didn't look around? No affairs?' I asked mischievously.

'Do you know Iqqy? Iqbal Singh. He was then living with me. The girls came to see me, but were entangled by Iqqy', Khushwant laughed.

He added: 'I came back. My father was very annoyed

with me. My wife was also annoyed with me. My father said, 'Look at this jerk. He got through his exams with difficulty. Didn't study the books prescribed in his course. Just...barely got through. And now he thinks he will write books!"

'My wife beseeched our common friends, 'Please put some sense into his head. He is a good-for-nothing, stupid fellow. What can a poor woman do?"

'So I left my house and went to Bhopal. My father had a factory there. I kept writing there. Then took my domestic helper with me and went to Kasauli and kept writing. Finished and gave finishing touches to *Train to Pakistan.* I got the American Global Press Award. I was loaded with admiration in India and abroad. The book got translated into several languages of the world.'

'One day an Englishman asked my father, 'Are you the father of Khushwant Singh? I would like to meet him.' So everybody thought that I had 'arrived'. I was accepted in the family, finally!'

'The prodigal son was accepted back in the fold!' I remarked.

'Exactly! Above all, my wife also accepted me. I got a job in UNESCO, Paris. After two years, I got rid of it and came back. For two years, I worked in All India Radio, though nobody actually does anything resembling 'work' in the radio. Everybody just strolls around', he said.

'And you couldn't accept any appointment, which did

not require hard work. The whole of your attention!' I asked again.

'Exactly! Then I had teaching assignments in America, in Oxford, in Tokyo', he said.

'And you were writing all along?' I asked.

'All the time. I used to get up at three in the morning. Those days, I was writing *The History of the Sikhs*,and translations of the sacred hymns from the *Guru Granth Sahib*. By breakfast time, I would complete the translation of one hymn. I felt I was on a high, intoxicated with the work. I felt the Guru's hand on my shoulder. I translated ,*Baramaah*, and *Jaap Sahib* portions of *Dasam Granth*.'

'For the History of the Sikhs, I got the Rockefeller Grant for three years. For one year, I got a grant from the Aligarh Muslim University to complete this work.

'After completing both the volumes, I wrote Opus Exegi in the end, two Latin words, which mean that 'my life's work has been completed."

'What do you feel like writing now?' I asked.

'I want to write a historical novel about *Delhi*, starting from Prithvi Raj Chauhan's period, to the assassination of Gandhi', he disclosed.

'History is always on a boil in this Delhi, always in the process of being chiselled. And Delhi chisels the history of the rest of the country,' he continued. Why ? up to the point of assassination of Gandhi ? Once you start writing, you can keep moving with the history, and go much beyond. There is only one person who can write this history: Khushwant Singh,' I said.

'There you are correct,' he said with a childlike conviction and serious honesty.

Honest with himself

'Khushwant, I feel you haven't done anything in life for which you have had to regret afterwards,' I remarked.

He contemplated seriously. As if he was trying to locate something from the past. 'Regret? I have never done anything for which I would feel ashamed before anybody. But before myself ...perhaps once or twice,' he confessed.

'Everybody can speak with aplomb about the marvellous things one has done in his life. But it needs a Khushwant Singh to confess something for which he felt ashamed,' I coaxed him.

He was serious and said, 'I have a friend in New York. Whenever I go there, I meet her.'

'Is she a mistress?' I smiled.

'No, just a friend,' he was very serious,'when I started meeting her, she had a little daughter,just like a doll. I used to carry her on my shoulders, and we played together. Gradually, she grew up. I never noticed. Whenever I went there, I still saw her like a little, doll-like girl.'

'Last year, I went to her home. I was sitting with my

friend when she received a phone call. Her daughter had met with an accident, and she was being driven to the hospital. They had asked the mother to reach the hospital immediately.'

'She got bewildered and very worried. I caught hold of her hand. She was trembling. I told her I would accompany her, and she shouldn't worry.'

'We rushed to the hospital. We came to know from the desk that she was in the First Aid room and was being looked after by the doctors. We rushed to the First Aid room. She was lying there, on the table. They had removed all her clothes, and were attending to her bruises. It was not serious. No bones had been broken, they informed us. In fact, she was in great shock.'

'We felt relieved. And then I started looking at her. For the first time' I realized that my doll had grown up into a beautiful young woman. As if one had kneaded saffron in milky white flour, white and pink,washed in dew, flawless! Her body was like God's own miracle, sheer beauty, a miracle.'

'And a burning desire travelled through my body. Oh my God, what was happening to me? What sort of hallucination was tormenting me?'

'I felt afterwards that it was a very dirty thought. I couldn't carry the burden of this guilt. So I told my friend. This confession wiped me clean.'

'I am proud of my writing. I felt very proud when I

conquered the heart of my Kawal who became my wife. And now I am proud of my granddaughter,' he smiled with genuine pride.

When he was a hero

'There is another incident I would like to share with you. Whenever I remember the incident, I am amazed how a coward like me could generate so much courage. That day, I had appeared for my interview for the foreign services. Those were the days of the Partition. I had just shifted to Delhi from Lahore. Those were very cruel times. Arson, looting and murders everywhere! I was passing Tees Hazari when I saw a crowd gathering and growing. I approached the crowd and saw that a mob had encircled two Muslims, who were holding the rope of a cow. There was a Sardar also with them. His turban had slipped to his chest. The mob was thrashing the Muslims and that Sardar too.'

'On inquiring into the matter, I came to know that the Sardar had sold off the cow to the two Muslims. The Sardar was beseeching them that he had nothing to do with the cow. They had unnecessarily implicated him.'

'I usually change my path whenever I see such a senseless mob. But I don't know what happened to me that day. I approached the centre of the mob, and abused and kicked that Sardar and made him run away. I wanted to do the same with the Muslims, but the mob didn't relent. The mob was bent on killing them. I argued with the mob, "Why do you want to take law into your own hands? Let us take them to the police station." The mob was in no mood to lose a chance of proving their valour.'

'I told them that I was a government official. It was not an exaggeration. I had been selected for the foreign services an hour back. But nobody was prepared to listen to me. The mob was very angry, and there was blood and arson in the air.'

'After much argument, I got hold of the cow's rope and said I was taking both the Muslims to the police station.'

'The SHO refused to file the complaint. He said, 'Somebody has sold the cow, and these men have bought it. What does the law have to do with this transaction?' I told him that my request was only to arrest the two Muslims, so that they are safe in the police custody. But he did not want to save them. He might have lost his home in Pakistan, or had been hurt by the arson and looting in Delhi.'

'I took them to another police station. I was leading, holding the rope of the cow, and those two Muslims followed me. Nobody adhered to my arguments even in the other police station. But by now, the mob following us had thinned. Hardly nine or ten people were still following us. They were also dead tired by now. Their anger had slowly evaporated. I left the rope dangling, and kicked the cow. She ran away. I argued a little with those people and they also sauntered away. I told them that I was taking both the Muslims to my home. In the backyard, I would kill them.'

'I took a cab and made them sit with me in the taxi. After reaching Daryaganj, I made the taxi stop and asked both of them to go home.

"When they were confident that they had actually been saved, they said. But Sardar jee, we lost our cow. This has been a great loss."

'After getting off the cab, I am sure they must have gone looking for the cow,' Khushwant said while concluding his story.

The stuff of history

When I reached his office at the *Hindustan Times* at the appointed time, I found him sitting there like a Peer, a Monarch, surrounded by star-struck students of journalism talking to him about politics and the socio-economic conditions in the country.

One of them asked, 'Why doesn't any evening news tabloid succeed?'

'Because news sweep in, are collected and graded in the evenings; published at night; and reach the people early morning. Even late night or midnight news are given prominence. It can be possible only in regular newspapers. There is hardly anything worthwhile to print in the evening news tabloids,' Khushwant explained to them.

'Is that why Mrs Indira Gandhi takes most of her most important decisions late night, or even at midnight?' one of them asked.

'Exactly! They make headlines the next morning. That is why I am also planning my departure somewhere in the middle of the night, so that obituaries should appear as headlines in all the papers the next morning', he chuckled like a naughty child. All of them laughed.

I felt devastated and depressed. A huge black cloud descended on me and engulfed me, suffocating me. That was Khushwant. He did make more than headlines. He made history. He was the stuff of history…

(The recollections of Khushwant Singh by Ajeet Caur have been taken from interviews and informal, leisurely talks over three or four months, in early 1981. They were published in April of that year and later published as the opening sketch in an Anthology of Sketches of important writers and creative minds: *'Takiye Daa Peer'*.)

Epilogue

Home they brought the warrior...

The poet Kaifi Azmi once said that, at the end of a man's life, his whole being longs to return to his roots, the land and the soil of his birth. 'Mitti bula-ti hai' (the earth and the dust call out to him)! It was certainly so with Khushwant. He had been born in the west Punjab village of Hadali, which is now in Pakistan. His boyhood and youth had been spent in Hadali and Lahore, and he had old friends there.

It was his wish that his ashes be taken to Hadali and kept there. In fact, in his last days, he had thought often about his death. He had written that it is an Indian trait to avoid all talk of death but, as far as he was concerned, he thought that, even as a man faces life, he must also face death. He found nothing morbid about it. In fact, as his son, Rahul Singh, has said, 'My father died a happy man.' Khushwant was in favour of the tradition of burial, as he felt that, 'in this way, you return back to the earth what came from the earth'. He had even gone to the Baha'i Temple in Delhi and selected a place where a grave could be made for him. He wanted his grave to be under the shade of a peepul tree. However, this could not be done.

His mortal remains were cremated in Delhi in the presence of his children and grandchild. He had written to his friends in Pakistan, among them the writer, FS Aijazuddin, expressing a wish that his ashes be taken to Hadali. This was done. He had last visited the village in 1987, when he had been warmly welcomed by the villagers. He had said to them: 'As you people go on pilgrimage to Mecca and Medina, coming back to Hadali at this time of evening in my life is my Haj pilgrimage…this is where my roots are and I have nourished them with tears of nostalgia.' Many generations of the villagers of Hadali had come and gone during the 99 years of Khushwant's life. But even the youngsters there had heard his name as the legend of the writer was remembered by the elders and passed on. Quite fittingly for a literary man, Khushwant's ashes were kept in the same school at Hadali, where he had studied as a child.

And so, after a life of 99 years, the old warrior was back in the village he had never forgotten. He was back among the sand dunes of Hadali, as the wild winds blew the restless sands far into the moonlit desert; back at the school, where he sat with other boys and chanted multiplication tables and wrote on wooden tablets. And once again, he was with his beloved grandmother in lazy summer afternoons in the courtyard of their village home, as she worked on her spinning wheel and chanted verses from the Scriptures.

He had been able to visit Hadali only thrice after he had moved to Delhi for his education. But it had stayed with him all his life. He had read the great books and the great ideas that men have formulated in an effort to understand life. He had written his own timeless and enduring books, and he had finally understood life, in all its beauty and its evanescence. There is not much else a man can do.

In one of his last interviews to a BBC team, Khushwant had spoken much about death and that he had done whatever he could have wanted. He had recited the poet Walter Savage Landor's lines in a firm voice:

I strove with none, for none was worth my strife;
Nature I loved, and next to Nature, Art.
I warmed my hands before the fire of life;
It sinks, and I am ready to depart.